Hope

Heaven's Own Gift

PAINTINGS BY

Sandy Lynam Clough

HARVEST HOUSE PUBLISHERS
EUGENE, OREGON

I wish for you faith...
I send to you hope...
I share with you love from a joyful heart.

—SANDY LYNAM CLOUGH

Hope—Heaven's Own Gift

Text Copyright © 2001 by Sandy Lynam Clough
Published by Harvest House Publishers
Eugene, Oregon 97402

ISBN 0-7369-0516-2

> Sandy Clough Studios
> 25 Trail Road
> Marietta, GA 30064
> 1.800.447.8409

Design and production by Garborg Design Works, Minneapolis, Minnesota

Scripture quotations are taken from the Holy Bible, New International
Version®, Copyright © 1973, 1978, 1984 by the International Bible Society.
Used by permission of Zondervan Publishing House; and the New King
James Version, Copyright © 1979, 1980, 1982 by Thomas Nelson, Inc.,
Publishers. Used by permission.

Printed in China.

00 01 02 03 04 05 06 07 08 09 / IM / 10 9 8 7 6 5 4 3 2 1

Every hope or dream
of the human mind will be
fulfilled if it is noble and of God.

OSWALD CHAMBERS

Hope is one of the greatest gifts we have been given by our heavenly Father. It carries no price tag but its value is priceless. We cling to it when the future looks uncertain and praise it when things turn out better than we could have ever imagined. Hope is the foundation on which we build our dreams and aspirations. It has been the cornerstone upon which ordinary people have accomplished extraordinary things.

Hope will always endure.

Hope

Sandy Lynam Clough

What oxygen is to the lungs,
such is hope to the meaning of life.

EMIL BRUNNER

Learn from yesterday,

live for today,

hope for tomorrow.

ANONYMOUS

May the God of hope fill you with
all joy and peace as you trust in Him,
so that you may overflow with hope...

THE BOOK OF ROMANS

Hope is a state of mind, not of the world. Hope,
in this deep and powerful sense, is not the same as joy
that things are going well, or willingness to invest in
enterprises that are obviously heading for success, but
rather an ability to work for something because it is good.

VACLAV HAVEL

*Hope is a risk
that must be run.*

GEORGES BERNANOS

*Be joyful in hope,
patient in affliction,
faithful in prayer.*

THE BOOK OF ROMANS

7

Man is, properly speaking, based upon hope,
he has no other possession but hope;
this world of his is emphatically the place of hope.

THOMAS CARLYLE

"Hope" is the thing with feathers—
That perches in the soul—
And sings the tune without the words—
And never stops—at all.

EMILY DICKINSON

Great hopes make great men.

THOMAS FULLER

Hope, like the gleaming taper's light,
Adorns and cheers our way;
And still, as darker grows the night,
Emits a brighter ray.

OLIVER GOLDSMITH

*He who has health,
has hope; and he who
has hope, has everything.*

PROVERB

And thus, oh Hope! Thy lovely form
In sorrow's gloomy night shall be
The sun that looks through cloud and storm
Upon a dark and moonless sea.

JOSEPH RODMAN DRAKE

Sandy Lynam Clough

It is difficult to say what is impossible,
for the dream of yesterday is the hope of today
and the reality of tomorrow.

ROBERT H. GODDARD

Never deprive someone of hope—
it may be all they have.

HENRY ADAMS

Be strong and take heart,
all you who hope in the LORD.

THE BOOK OF PSALMS

Take short views,
hope for the best,
and trust in God.

SYDNEY SMITH

Entertain great hopes.

ROBERT FROST

Hope is a gift we give ourselves,
and it remains when all else is gone.

NAOMI JUDD

Hope sees the invisible, feels the intangible
and achieves the impossible.

AUTHOR UNKNOWN

Such is hope, heaven's own gift to
struggling mortals, pervading,
like some subtle essence from the skies,
all things both good and bad.

CHARLES DICKENS

The capacity for hope is the most significant fact of life.
It provides human beings with a sense of
destination and the energy to get started.

NORMAN COUSINS

Please come for tea —
Sandy

As long as we have hope, we have direction, the energy to move, and the map to move by. We have a hundred alternatives, a thousand paths and an infinity of dreams. Hopeful, we are halfway to where we want to go; hopeless, we are lost forever.

AUTHOR UNKNOWN

We live by admiration,
hope and love.

WILLIAM WORDSWORTH

We judge of man's
wisdom by his hope.

RALPH WALDO EMERSON

Optimism is the faith that leads to achievement.
Nothing can be done without hope and confidence.

HELEN KELLER

Hope is a strange invention—
A Patent of the Heart—
In unremitting action
Yet never wearing out.

EMILY DICKINSON

Hope is some extraordinary spiritual grace that
God gives us to control our fears, not to oust them.

VINCENT MCNABB

The word which God has written on the brow of every man is Hope.

Hope is like the sun, which,
as we walk toward it, casts a shadow
of our burdens behind us.

ANONYMOUS

And now these three remain: faith, hope and love.

THE BOOK OF 1 CORINTHIANS

Hope is both the earliest and the most indispensable
virtue inherent in the state of being alive.
If life is to be sustained hope must remain,
even where confidence is wounded, trust impaired.

ERIK H. ERIKSON

Sandy Lynam Clough

23

Now faith is the substance of things hoped for,
the evidence of things not seen.

THE BOOK OF HEBREWS

Hope is the parent of faith.

CYRUS A. BARTOL

We must accept
finite disappointment,
but never lose infinite hope.

MARTIN LUTHER KING JR.

Three grand
essentials to happiness
in this life are
something to do,
something to love,
and something
to hope for.

JOSEPH ADDISON

A strong defense to guard the soul
Is ours from heaven above;
God fills our hearts with steadfast hope
And gives us faith and love.

DENNIS DeHANN

Men and women are limited not by the place of their birth, not by the color of their skin, but by the size of their hope.

JOHN JOHNSON

Each time a person stands
up for an ideal, or acts to improve the
lot of others, or strikes out against injustice,
he sends forth a tiny ripple of hope.

ROBERT FRANCIS KENNEDY

*Everything that is done
in the world is done by hope.*

MARTIN LUTHER

Hope is the pillar that holds up the world.
Hope is the dream of a waking man.

PLINY

Sandy Lynam Clough 29

Sandy Lynam Clough

My hope arises from the freeness of grace, and not from the freedom of the will.

Hope is itself a species of happiness, and, perhaps, the chief happiness which this world affords.

DR. SAMUEL JOHNSON

Always be prepared to
give an answer to everyone
who asks you to give the reason
for the hope that you have.

THE BOOK OF 1 PETER

Nurse Crawford's Peril

NURSE
CRAWFORD'S
PERIL

Evelyn Martin

AVALON BOOKS
THOMAS BOUREGY AND COMPANY, INC.
NEW YORK

PRINTED IN THE UNITED STATES OF AMERICA
BY HADDON CRAFTSMEN, SCRANTON, PENNSYLVANIA

Nurse Crawford's Peril

CHAPTER ONE

Dee Crawford was surprised to find how tired she felt as she entered the office of her doctor, Helen Irons. The reason for her visit was twofold. Helen had indicated she might have a nursing job lined up for Dee, and Dee felt she needed a general checkup after the last few exhausting months nursing her widowed mother around the clock until she passed away from a final stroke.

Dee caught sight of her reflection in a mirror on the wall of the waiting room and realized she looked almost as tired as she felt. She had lost a lot of weight recently, which made her high cheekbones more apparent. Her brown hair, with its highlights of gold, showed evidence of neglect, and her large brown eyes, usually so merry, seemed lifeless and dull.

1

As she entered Dr. Irons's inner office, the sight of the pink-cheeked, gray-haired woman in her crisp white jacket made Dee feel better. Helen had been an old and dear friend of the family, and she had attended Alice Crawford, Dee's mother, during her final illness.

Helen looked up at Dee and smiled, her eyes bright above her rimless spectacles. "Come in and sit down, Dee. I'm assuming you're ready to go back to work."

Dee shrugged philosophically. "I don't really have a choice, do I? Mother's illness ate up most of Dad's insurance, so now it's up to me to earn my own living."

Dr. Irons eyed her sympathetically. "I'm proud of you, Dee. Not many girls would have given up a nursing post on the staff of a fine hospital like Wilson General to devote themselves completely to a dying mother. You made these last months much easier for Alice."

"I'm glad," Dee said simply. "I loved her, you know."

Helen Irons nodded, looking with fondness at the sweet-faced girl before her. She could remember Dee's graduation from nursing school. Helen had been instrumental in helping the girl get her post at Wilson

General Hospital a short time later. Dee had made a fine nurse, too. Dedicated and responsible.

"I think I have a job for you that's just what you need right now," Helen said abruptly. "Of course, I intend to give you a thorough physical before I let you commit yourself to anything, but I'm sure all I'll find is an exhausted girl who needs some rest and vitamins and sunshine." She reached into a manila folder and extracted a letter. "I have here a communication from a colleague of mine, a Dr. Stephen Winthrop. He needs a live-in nurse for a patient in rather isolated circumstances, and I think the job might be just the thing for you."

"I had thought maybe I would ask for my old job back at Wilson General," Dee said hesitantly.

"I wouldn't like to see you place yourself under that heavy work load immediately," Helen said in a discouraging tone. "On Wakeford Island, you'll have only the one patient, leaving time for you to sunbathe and swim and get a good rest. As a matter of fact, I've already told Steve about you and he seems quite enthusiastic."

Dee leaned back in the hard chair, thinking it sounded too good to be true. There had to be a catch somewhere. "Tell me about the patient," she said.

Helen referred to her notes briefly. "He's an old man of eighty-one. Not long ago, he suffered a stroke. His speech has returned sufficiently so that he can express his needs, but he does require regular care and continued therapy. Luckily, he has the money to pay for it. His name is Nicholas Wakeford —hence, Wakeford Island."

"Does he have a family?"

"Not in residence. The only people Steve mentioned were a housekeeper, a Mrs. Eileen Powers, and her son, Bert, who acts as a caretaker for the estate. I'm sure there are other people around, but Steve didn't go into any detail. The island is off the Florida mainland, in the Gulf of Mexico, less than fifty miles from here. Shall I set up an appointment for you to talk to Steve about the job?"

Slowly Dee nodded. "It sounds too good to be true."

After examining Dee and giving her a clean bill of health, the doctor said, "I'll leave you to dress while I see if I can reach Steve."

A few minutes later, Helen came bustling in. "I managed to find Steve," she said cheerfully. "He's in something of a hurry, so he suggested he pick you up tonight and you could discuss the case over dinner." She paused guiltily. "I took the liberty of telling him that would be fine. Gave him your address. You don't mind, do you? He'll be there at seven-fifteen."

Dee grinned reluctantly. "Now, wait a minute, Dr. Helen. Just how old is this colleague of yours?"

Helen said, "Oh, about thirty-five, unmarried, with a gorgeous physique, a shock of sandy hair, and hazel eyes."

Dee sputtered indignantly, "This better not be another of your matchmaking schemes!"

Helen raised innocent eyes. "Me? Of course not. As I said, this is exactly the kind of job you need right now."

Once Dee had returned to the empty house, she busied herself going through her wardrobe until the time neared for her dinner date with Dr. Stephen Winthrop. Though she had no idea whether she would be hired, or even if she would take the job offered to her, she decided it wouldn't hurt to be prepared.

She pulled out her uniforms, making sure they were all fresh and in good condition. She selected only a few dresses that would be suitable for any off-hours on the island, not forgetting plenty of casual clothing and a bathing suit. Her other things she packed away, getting them ready for storage, for the Crawford house was going up for sale. It was much too large for Dee. She had already arranged to have the few items she really treasured put away until she found a smaller place to live. Right now she was not sure she would stay in the town of Wilson or even in Florida.

Flipping through the dresses that were left, Dee selected a simple lime-green cotton sheath that flattered her figure. After taking a relaxing bath, she got dressed and carefully applied her makeup.

Dr. Winthrop was right on time. When Dee heard the doorbell, she closed her eyes for a moment and breathed a silent prayer that the doctor would accept her for the assignment so her life might be resolved, at least for a few months.

She swung open the front door to see a tall young man who was quite attractive with his sandy hair, bronzed skin, and hazel eyes.

"Dee Crawford?" he inquired, smiling warmly. "Helen Irons set up our dinner date. I hope the notice wasn't too short for you."

He flushed slightly and forced himself to slow down. "Oh, by the way, I'm Stephen Winthrop."

Dee graciously said, "How do you do, Dr. Winthrop. Won't you come in?"

She stood aside to let him enter. He seemed very big and masculine in the neat living room.

"I'm afraid we may have to hurry a bit," he apologized. "The only reservation I could get was for seven-thirty."

"No problem," she said. "I'm all ready."

She reached for her bag and preceded him to the trim red sports car in the driveway. As he closed the door on her side, she sank back into the luxurious leather upholstery. Apparently, Dr. Stephen Winthrop was rather successful.

"You look much younger than I was led to expect," he said abruptly as he pulled into the traffic. "And much prettier."

"I assure you I'm an experienced nurse," she told him stiffly. "You can get my references from Wilson General Hospital."

"That really wasn't the thing that was bothering me," he told her frankly. "You see, Wakeford Island can be a rather lonely place, and it's hard to see a young woman like you being happy there for any length of time.

Once I get Nicholas settled with you, I'd hate to upset his routine again."

"I assure you I'll carry out any commitment I make," she said. "But I would like to know a little more about the patient. If he requires constant nursing care, why is he on his island? Wouldn't it be simpler to put him in a nursing facility?"

Stephen chuckled. "First, you don't put Nicholas anywhere. The old goat does just as he pleases. Right now it pleases him to be home. He can afford to hire the help he needs, and it isn't that hard for me to run over from the mainland to look in on him. I imagine we'll need you at least four months—then play it by ear."

"Dr. Irons says there's a housekeeper."

"Yes. Eileen Powers. A possessive, evil old witch, but she's been with Nicholas for years and feels she owns him." He seemed thoughtful. "Then there's her son, Bert, who acts as caretaker. He's a sullen, brooding young man who resents being trapped on the island. Mrs. Powers sees to hiring the other help. They come and they go. You'll have to be self-sufficient to deal with that household."

"I don't see why I should have any problems if I approach the matter with a professional attitude," Dee said.

"I just wouldn't like you to have any un-expected surprises." He swung the car into a driveway, and Dee recognized the parking lot of one of the nicest restaurants in Wilson.

Inside, it was evident that Stephen Winthrop was known. They were escorted to a table by a window that looked out over the water, where darkness was just falling.

"Tell me more about Nicholas Wakeford," Dee asked after they had ordered. "Just how much care does he need?"

"He's mobile, but he walks with a cane. Needs some physical therapy. Requires a lot of rest, and it's important that he take his medication regularly. He has suffered one mild stroke and has made a remarkable comeback for a man of eighty-one. He's irascible on occasion, but very alert. Your main problem would be seeing that he gets sufficient rest and doesn't overdo with alcohol or cigars."

"That doesn't seem so difficult," Dee said slowly. "Doesn't he have any family at all?"

Stephen smiled grimly. "One grandson, Jason Wakeford. They can't seem to get along. Too much alike. Jason pops up periodically to see about the old man, but it always ends with the two of them in a big row. They can't seem to agree on anything."

The waiter brought their food, and Dee found that she was hungry. They limited their conversation to small talk until they were done and the white-jacketed waiter had poured their coffee.

"I enjoyed that," Dee said. "I was hungry."

"So was I," the young doctor said. "And your companionship added just the right touch to a lovely meal. All right, Miss Dee Crawford, you have the job."

"Thank you." She felt a faint relief, having her immediate future settled.

He looked at her curiously. "Dee sounds like a nickname. What's the real one?"

"Dyelle. An old family name, shortened long ago for convenience."

"An unusual name for an unusual girl." He looked deep into her eyes and raised his coffee cup. "Here's to a long and pleasant relationship."

Dee smiled and raised her cup in return, meeting his eyes with her own.

He suddenly asked, "Are you sure there won't be a lot of disappointed swains pining away for you here on the mainland?"

She shook her head firmly. "Not a one, Dr. Winthrop. I've been a bit too busy for romance."

The eyes burning into hers told her he

didn't quite believe her. She was glad. Dr. Stephen Winthrop was an attractive man, and she felt a little tingle in her spine at the frank admiration in his eyes.

"I'll be making my usual visit to the island this weekend," he said. "I'll pick you up at your place Friday afternoon at five. We'll have to drive down to Galena to catch the launch they'll send over for us. I'll call Bert to be there to meet us."

"I'll have everything ready," she promised.

Dee sensed that Stephen hated to have the evening end, but it was time to leave the restaurant. She offered him coffee when they were back at her house, but he declined. Still, his hand lingered on hers as he bade her good night, and Dee found her heart beating a little more rapidly when the door closed behind him.

As she dropped her handbag on the hall table, she slowly looked about her. This had been her home all of her life. She hated giving it up, but the time had come when she must. She had already put it into the hands of realtors, and it might well be sold while she was on the island.

Wakeford Island. It sounded so isolated. Just what was she getting into? A testy old man, a resentful housekeeper, a sullen son. Well, at least it would be a challenge. It was better to change everything in her life now that her mother was gone.

Dee had conquered her grief, put it behind her. It was time to start her own life, venturing into it bravely, facing whatever it might bring.

CHAPTER TWO

Dee efficiently took care of countless details in the next few days. The drive to Galena was very pleasant in the late afternoon
on Friday. Stephen had put the top of his
sports car down, and the warm Florida wind
ruffled Dee's hair, soothing her with gently
massaging fingers.

They skirted the little town of Galena and
pulled up in a parking lot near the wharf.
While Steve put the top up on the car and
began to carry their luggage to the wharf,
Dee went in search of a rest room where she
could comb her tumbled hair and freshen
her makeup.

She found one in a little bait shop built
right on the wharf. There was only one girl
working inside, a flaxen-haired, slender

young woman in jeans and a heavy apron. She pointed the way to the rest room, and it only took a moment for Dee to freshen up and return to the counter.

Looking through the window of the bait shop, Dee could see that the launch was not yet near the wharf.

A brightly colored rack of postcards caught her eye. Among them she spotted a series that featured aerial views of a small island, set like a jewel in the sea. Turning one of the cards over, she saw that the caption said: "Wakeford Island, privately owned by Nicholas C. Wakeford, a philanthropist and industrialist who has been prominent in the area surrounding Galena."

"I'll take a few of these," Dee told the girl. "This is where I'm going. I'm surprised to find it's well-known enough to be featured on a postcard."

Reluctantly the girl took the cards from her, saying, "Take my advice, and don't go. Surely, you can find work somewhere else."

"What do you mean?" Dee asked curiously.

"It's a horrible place to work. Take my word for it. Did Mrs. Powers hire you? Around here we call her the witch of Wakeford Island. And that son of hers! He still gives me the creeps! I only worked there three months, but, believe me, that was enough!"

Dee gave the young woman a bill from her wallet and pocketed the change. "Fortunately, I wasn't hired by Mrs. Powers. I'm a private nurse, and I'll be taking care of Mr. Wakeford."

"He's a nasty old man, too, always whining and complaining. You can't do anything right for those people. Mark my words, nurse or not, you'll soon be on that launch coming back here, and glad to get away!"

Dee smiled. "Thanks for the advice. When I come back, I'll drop by to see you, and we can compare notes."

"You'll be glad to get away, too. You'll see!"

Dee slipped the cards she had purchased into her purse and went outside to find Steve had transferred all their luggage to the end of the pier where a long, sleek launch now lay at anchor.

At first, as she approached, Dee didn't think there was anybody on board, but then she saw the dark, stocky young man coming up from the galley.

Dee realized the young man must be Bert Powers. He had a broad face, with dark eyes under thick brows and a shock of dark hair.

He was dressed in faded denims, an old T-shirt, and deck shoes. He nodded curtly to Stephen without speaking, ignoring Dee as though she were not there.

Steve reached out a hand to help her climb on board as Bert passed them, jumping lithely onto the weather-beaten wharf. Dee watched Bert as he picked up their bags and effortlessly brought them aboard in one load, as though they weighed nothing, and then stowed them away in the cabin.

When Bert came over to them, Steve put one hand on his brawny forearm and said, "Bert, I'd like you to meet Dee Crawford, who is going to the island as Mr. Wakeford's nurse. Dee, this is Bert Powers, the care-taker of the estate."

"Hello." Dee tried to smile brightly, but Bert merely touched his forelock in greet-ing, with no word at all.

Steve kept his grasp on the young man's arm. "Ready to cast off, Bert?"

Bert shook his head and brushed Steve's hand away at the same time. "Nope. Got to wait."

"May I ask why?" Steve said.

"Got to wait for Kennedy."

"Wakeford's lawyer? Don't tell me the old man's changing his will again."

Bert shrugged. "How would I know?" His eyes were focused on the railing, past Steve's shoulder. "Why don't you ask him yourself? Here he comes now."

Dee took one look and told herself that Nicholas Wakeford certainly surrounded himself with good-looking people! The lawyer's head was covered with a crown of close-cropped golden curls, and his eyes were the same beautiful blue as a spring sky. His skin was the same dark bronze of most Floridians, and his smile was infectious above the faint cleft in his chin.

"Hello, Steve," he said cheerfully. "Sorry I'm late. Got delayed in court." He stopped still when he spotted Dee and surveyed her carefully. "And who is this vision of beauty?"

"My colleague, Dee Crawford, who is to be Nicholas's nurse," Steve answered stiffly. "Dee, meet Paul Kennedy, Nicholas's attorney, as you've no doubt gathered."

"My pleasure!" Paul drew nearer and took Dee's hand in both of his. "A nurse, are you? I've never seen anybody less cold and clinical in my life."

"I have my moments," Dee answered.

"I'll bet you do." Paul swept her to the side of the boat, offering her a seat as though it were a throne.

Glancing at Steve, Dee noticed his eyes held a veiled amusement, as well as a touch of hostility. Apparently, there was no love lost between these two men.

The launch motor roared to life, then settled down to a smooth purr when the boat left the pier. The wake extended behind them in a smooth vee as the craft headed into the sunset. Dee's hair whipped against her cheeks in the sea breeze, and she inhaled deeply, loving the fresh air, enjoying this moment between the day and the evening, with darkness stealing over the Gulf.

Dee had always enjoyed the water. Now she found the slight pitch of the waves exhilarating, the smell of the salt in the air tantalizing and mysterious. Bert turned on the running lights, and she realized with amazement that darkness had almost completely fallen. They were alone in the vast expanse of ocean in their frail craft.

Steve and Paul were engaged in conversation, so Dee took the opportunity to move away from them toward the bow, where she could look down into the water and try to shake off the tension she felt at the prospect of meeting her new employer.

She really wasn't aware of how long she sat there before she felt Steve touch her shoulder lightly. "There it is," he said, pointing to a twinkle of lights far out in the darkness. "Wakeford Island."

Steve was so close, Dee could feel his breath against her ear, and she found his nearness comforting. She was aware of the faint, tangy scent of his aftershave, which was clean and fresh.

Dee found herself wishing he were going to be a permanent fixture on the island, but she knew that as soon as he had established her duties, he would go away again, probably tomorrow or Sunday. She knew she was going to feel terribly alone when he left her by herself to cope with Nicholas.

Dee was aware of Paul coming to join them. He sat down beside her. "I take it this is your first visit to the island?"

She nodded, brushing back the hair that was blowing over her eyes.

"It's lovely," Paul said. "I'm sure you're going to enjoy working there, if you can just handle old Nick."

She smiled. "No problem," she said positively. "I'm a regular tyrant when I'm on duty."

"Someone so pretty could never be tyrannical," he replied flirtatiously.

It made Dee faintly uncomfortable. Paul

seemed to be a little too sure of his charm and good looks, and obviously used them to his own advantage.

Dee could see the faint outline of the island wharf now and the looming palm trees dark against the moonlit sky. Soon the motor grew silent and the launch moved smoothly up to the pier. Bert leaped out to make the boat fast. Then Steve offered Dee his assistance in leaving the launch.

Once they were across the wharf, Dee felt the crisp crunch of white oyster shells under her feet and noticed the shelled road led into the interior of the island.

There was a jeep parked off to the side, and Bert loaded their luggage into the back quickly and efficiently. Though it was dark, the island seemed to teem with life. Dee could hear little rustlings in the verdant growth about her, and she found herself glad she wouldn't be on foot in this unfamiliar territory.

She found herself in the back seat with Steve, while Paul got in front with Bert. Dee felt the lawyer did so with reluctance. As the jeep wended its way up the curving road, Dee could see a bit of the thick growth about them in the pale light cast by the moon.

They were at the house before she knew it. It was a long, rambling place, with only

a few lights burning. There seemed to be
several added-on wings. Dee felt her heart
pounding with sudden trepidation. This was
to be her home for the next few months at
least. Inside were her patient, Nicholas
Wakeford, and his dragon of a housekeeper,
Eileen Powers.

Dee steadied her nerves by reminding
herself that she was here in a purely professional capacity and need take orders from
no one but Dr. Stephen Winthrop.

The door was opened by a tall, thin woman
who stared at them insolently, no show of
welcome in her eyes. The dim hall light cast
menacing shadows across her face, empha-
sizing her coldness. Her dark hair was drawn
back into an unflattering bun, and her pale-
blue eyes seemed dead and lifeless.

"I wasn't expecting so many people," she
said sharply.

Paul gave her an engaging smile. "I wasn't
supposed to come until next week," he explained, "but Nicholas called me to come
earlier, so here I am!"

"So I see," Mrs. Powers replied shortly.

Steve stepped forward, pulling Dee with
him. "Mrs. Powers, this is Miss Dee Crawford. She's been hired as a private nurse for
Mr. Wakeford."

Dee started to thrust out her hand, but

the woman turned away. "I'm aware of that,"
she sniffed. "Though why I can't care for
him as I've always done is a mystery to me."

"He needs professional help just now,"
Steve said firmly. "I thought I explained that
to you already."

"You're the doctor." The housekeeper
turned and moved stiffly toward the back
of the house. "Come on in, and I'll see if I
can manage accommodations for all of you."

Steve gave Dee's hand a reassuring
squeeze as they followed the spare figure.
Paul mumbled something beneath his
breath, and Dee saw Eileen Powers's shoulders stiffen, though she did not break her
stride.

Entering a long hall with several doors
on each side, Eileen deposited Paul in the
first and Steve in the second on one side,
then opened one of the doors across the hall
for Dee.

"Mr. Wakeford is right next door," she explained tersely. "I may have to change your
accommodations later, but this will have to
do for now. The other rooms aren't fixed up
for visitors right now."

"Thank you," Dee said.

Mrs. Powers had turned on the lights, and
Dee entered, finding the room rather large.

Eileen Powers turned at the door, tucking her long slender hands under her apron. "Bert will deliver your bags shortly. There'll be a meal served in exactly forty minutes. Please be prompt. I detest tardiness."

"I'll be there."

The woman's attitude set Dee's teeth on edge. Eileen Powers seemed to carry a perpetual chip on her shoulder.

The housekeeper's eyes flicked over Dee's windblown appearance disdainfully. "You might make yourself presentable," she said. "You'll find a private bath off this room. It's possible you might be meeting Mr. Wakeford later tonight."

"I'll see to it."

The woman was really unpleasant. Dee was glad when the opening door revealed Bert bringing her bags up from the jeep. He tossed them on the bed without a word. When he left, Eileen Powers followed him out.

Dee breathed a sigh of relief. What a distasteful pair! Now at last she had an opportunity to look around her.

The room was spacious, with one wall of windows and glass doors that opened on a terrace. The bedroom itself was decorated in warm earth colors, from the russet carpet to the beige spread on the huge bed. Though the furniture seemed more masculine than feminine, it was quite attractive and very expensive.

Dee found the two closets empty and busied herself hanging up her uniforms and the other clothes she had brought with her. After she had placed the rest of her things into empty drawers and put away her suitcases in the bottom of the bigger closet, she glanced at her watch and found twenty of her precious minutes had passed away.

Experience had taught her discipline. There was a shower in the neat brown-and-white bath, and in a remarkably short time the rosy, sun-kissed girl had disappeared and been replaced by the starched, efficient Nurse Crawford.

Dee was just in time, for a sharp rap sounded on her door. She opened it to find Dr. Winthrop outside, waiting to escort her to dinner. He, too, had changed and was wearing a white sport shirt with an open collar and neat white slacks. He smiled as he saw her uniform.

"Sure you aren't rushing things a bit?" he asked pleasantly.

She smiled back at him. "Mrs. Powers hinted I change, since I might be meeting my patient this evening."

He took her arm, steering her toward the end of the hall. "Dear Mrs. Powers," he murmured ruefully. "She remains the resident dragon."

"I won't let her intimidate me," Dee promised him.

"I can believe that," he said. "You seem extremely capable of taking care of yourself."

When they reached the dining room, Paul was already there, his hair still damp from his shower. The bright golden curls clustered like a halo around his head.

The informal dining room included a long oak table and cane chairs. A low bowl of white camellias formed a centerpiece flanked by white candles in silver holders. Dee had expected that she might meet Nicholas Wakeford at dinner, but looking around the room, she could see no evidence that he would be there. Apparently, he did not take his meals with the others.

Neither did either Mrs. Powers or Bert. The housekeeper served a plain but delicious meal, and Dee found the two men to be delightful companions. She still felt an underlying tension between them, however. There seemed to be many things unsaid, a disturbing atmosphere of strain, and a general sense that Paul Kennedy and Stephen

Winthrop did not like each other.

Dee was relieved when dinner was over and Mrs. Powers served their coffee. Before Paul could finish his, Mrs. Powers came back into the room, pausing by his chair officiously.

"Mr. Wakeford requests your presence immediately, Mr. Kennedy," she said sharply.

Paul sighed and got to his feet. He must have brought his briefcase to dinner with him, for now he lifted it from a chair by the buffet. After apologizing to his companions, he followed the housekeeper out of the room.

"Apparently, Mr. Wakeford is in a hurry to see his attorney," Dee remarked.

Steve shook his head. "Nicholas plays games with Paul. As you may have gathered, he has quite an extensive estate. And business interests involving textiles, chemicals, automobile equipment, and on and on. Paul had been handling his affairs for years. Nicholas keeps everybody around him in line by periodically threatening to change his will."

Dee looked surprised. "How can that be a problem? From what I understand, there can't be that many heirs."

"There are a lot of people who'd like to be," Steve said wryly. "I'm afraid Nick doesn't get along well with his grandson, Jason. They're always on tenterhooks with each other. Mrs. Powers expects to inherit a good chunk of the estate. Some people think she has something on the old man, and she's been with him for years. She even expects Bert to share in the will, for he grew up with Jason, and he's stayed here on the island to care for the old man. Paul has a good stake in it, too, and he likes to look out for his own interests."

"And you?" Dee questioned. She couldn't help giving vent to her curiosity.

"Me?" Steve laughed. "I'm only his doctor. I have no desire to get involved in the devious plots that surround Mr. Nicholas Wakeford."

"I met a young woman in the bait shop back in Galena who warned me very strongly against coming here to work."

Steve chuckled. "I imagine Galena is full of disgruntled young women who have tried to work here. Can you imagine being at Eileen Powers's beck and call? It's no wonder they leave here in droves."

A sound at the door made them turn. It was Paul returning from his interview with Nicholas Wakeford.

"That didn't take long," the lawyer said

brusquely, reaching for the silver coffeepot to refill his cup. "True to form, he wants to revise the old will again. I can keep one secretary busy just doing his typing. We agreed to iron out the details tomorrow. Meanwhile, he wants to see you, Steve, and meet the nurse you've hired for him." He turned to Dee. "Good luck!"

"I don't think Dee will need it," Steve said matter-of-factly. "She has too much going for her." He extended his hand, helping Dee to her feet. "Shall we go and beard the lion in his den?"

Dee nodded, flashing him a quick smile. "After you, Doctor."

As they made their way through the hall to Nicholas's bedroom, Dee found her nerves tightening. Sternly she told herself that Nicholas Wakeford was only another patient and she would not allow him to intimidate her. Still, few patients had had the buildup that Nicholas Wakeford had been given.

Steve rapped at the closed door and announced himself with a terse, "Winthrop."

He was answered by a gruff voice that bade him come in.

Nicholas Wakeford was indeed a virtual lion of a man. He sat in a wine bathrobe by a table, his gnarled hands crossed on the

silver handle of a cane he had perched between his knees. A mane of silver hair
sprang from a broad brow above bushy eyebrows of the same hue. Dee noticed that his
pale-blue eyes were still sharp and alert.

"So you're my new nurse, are you?" He
looked Dee up and down, and she felt like
a butterfly impaled on a pin. The craggy
face was interesting, and his voice was
slurred only a little from the light stroke he
had suffered.

"That's right," Dee said firmly, stepping
forward with her hand outstretched. "And
I hope we're going to be friends."

He drew away from her, shaking his head
like an angry old bull. "Don't fuss over me,
woman! I can't bear to be fussed over!"

"I have no intention of fussing over you,"
Dee said. "But I may do a bit of fussing at
you if you don't obey Dr. Winthrop's orders.
I'm here to see you get better, and I intend
to do just that."

Nicholas's eyes twinkled at Steve. "Feisty
little cuss, isn't she?"

"You won't put much over on her," Steve
said.

"I won't be spied on!" the old man said
angrily. "I'll do what I please with what is
mine."

"And why shouldn't you?" Dee reached

out for his wrist and casually began to take his pulse. "I'm only interested in your physical well-being. Getting yourself into a temper tantrum won't help you at all, you know."

"I've made up my mind," Nicholas stated firmly, but his eyes were clouded as though he were talking to himself. "I'm going to put an end to this bickering once and for all."

"Right now I think we'd better get you into bed, so I can brief Miss Crawford on your schedule and medications. Give me a hand, Dee."

Between them, they helped the old man to his feet and into the big four-poster bed that dominated the room.

For the next hour, Dee had her hands full. She took notes of everything she was to do for Nicholas. Steve was giving him a light sleeping medication, and Dee was relieved when the old man closed his eyes and went to sleep at last.

"Should I look in on him later?" she asked when they had left the room.

"It might be a good idea. Meanwhile, I'll have Mrs. Powers show you the house, so you'll know where to find the things you need. And in case I forgot to mention it, Nick has a silver bell he can ring if he needs you."

Paul appeared to be awaiting Dee's return

avidly and seemed disappointed when she spent most of the evening with Steve and Mrs. Powers.

Dee found she was very tired when she finally reached her bed to spend her first night on Wakeford Island.

CHAPTER THREE

Dee found it difficult to go to sleep once she had slipped between the fresh sheets. The happenings of the day kept coming back to haunt her. This was a strange household. She really had no problem with Nicholas. He was old and cantankerous, but she felt she could handle him. He was fretting and upset about something, though, and she wished it was resolved. Worry was the last thing he needed.

Eileen Powers was a cold, unfriendly woman. Dee wondered if she showed the same face to Nicholas, then decided that couldn't be. Nicholas would never keep her on if she were that disagreeable to him.

Bert Powers was almost frightening. He was a mass of pent-up anger, and Dee felt

sure he could be dangerous if strongly pro-
voked. And Paul Kennedy was something
of a mystery. Dee never trusted men who
seemed to like her too much too soon.

Yet Stephen Winthrop seemed to be just
what he was supposed to be—a doctor and
a gentleman. Dee found him enormously attractive and couldn't help wondering if he
saw her as a woman as well as a nurse. She
hoped he did. He had certainly given some
signs of it.

The curtains at the windows were thin,
and Dee could see the swaying trees outside.
Gnarled and twisted, festooned with dripping moss, they looked like menacing,
bearded old men out of nightmares. Somehow their undulations seemed ominous, and
she turned her back to the windows and
French doors.

Wakeford Island. Dee was on a speck out
in the Gulf, completely surrounded by water,
and the only way she could get back to the
mainland was on the launch with the disagreeable Bert Powers. She felt very alone.

Finally, exhaustion took over and she slept
restlessly. But not for long.

Suddenly, she was awake and shivering.
There was a cool breeze blowing across her
body from the open glass doors, and she

gasped as she saw the dark figure of a man crossing the floor, his shadow outlined against the gray squares of the windows. Dee thought at first she must be dreaming. But the reality of the situation came home to her as the intruder threw something heavy on the bed at her feet, and she winced.

She was just about to scream for help when harsh light flooded the room. Dee sat up and clutched the covers around her, realizing that her midnight visitor was just as surprised as she was.

He was standing by the light switch, scowling, his face like a thundercloud. Black curly hair fell over his forehead, and fiery dark eyes stared into her own.

"What the hell are you doing here?" he asked, outraged.

"I might ask you the same thing," Dee retorted sharply. She could see now that the heavy object he had thrown on the foot of the bed was a bulging suitcase.

"This happens to be *my* bedroom," he snapped. "Always has been."

"Then you tell Mrs. Powers that. She's the one who put me here. Would you mind explaining just who you are and what you're doing here?"

He let his tall frame collapse into a ma-

hogany chair that sat beside a Queen Anne
desk. "I'm Jason Wakeford, and this is my
home. Now would you tell me what you're
doing here?"

"I'm Dee Crawford, and I've been hired as
a private nurse for Nicholas Wakeford," she
said.

He eyed her sharply. "How is the old boy?"

"As well as can be expected, with all the
odd things that go on around here," she answered. "Did he know you were coming?"

"I dropped him a line. I've been out of the
country. I just heard he had suffered a stroke
and came here immediately. I only hope the
sight of me doesn't trigger another one."
Jason sighed raggedly.

Dee gestured toward the chair where she
had draped her robe. "Would you give me
my robe, please?" She kept the covers up
high.

He lifted the thin cotton robe in two fingers and turned away as she slipped into it.
Once it was belted about her, and she had
slipped her feet into her slippers, she felt
better fortified to face this stranger in the
night.

She found he was much taller than she
was. In fact, she had to look up to meet his
eyes.

"I'm very sorry you've been inconvenienced," Dee said politely. "Maybe, if we wake Mrs. Powers, she can find me another place to sleep. Obviously, she wasn't expecting you."

"Mrs. Powers is not one of my favorite people," Jason answered shortly. "And I'm not in the habit of informing her of my movements."

"Well, it's obvious that something will have to be done, Mr. Wakeford, if either of us is to get any sleep," Dee said.

He continued as though she had not interrupted him. "Also, I wish you'd call me Jason. Around here, we reserve the Mr. Wakefords for old Nick."

"Very well, Jason. However, it becomes increasingly clear that some other arrangements will have to be made."

He flopped back down in his chair, and suddenly he looked like a sulky little boy. "There's a couch in my old playroom I can use, so don't worry about it. I suppose I've been ungracious, but I've had a long trip, I'm tired and I'm hungry, and I didn't expect to find a strange woman in my bed."

"How did you get here from the mainland?" Dee asked curiously.

"I have my own boat docked in the marina

at Galena. I like to furnish my own trans-
portation to the island. If Bert had to bring
me over from the mainland, I wouldn't be a
bit surprised if he capsized the boat."

Dee glanced at him sharply. "You're jok-
ing, of course."

He smiled ruefully. "I only wish I were.
Bert cares for me only a little less than his
mother does." Jason rose and reached for
his suitcase. "The least I can do is get out
of your way and let you have a decent night's
rest. I apologize for giving you such a rude
awakening."

Dee put out a hand to stay him. "You said
you were hungry, Jason. Why don't you let
me make you a sandwich and a cup of coffee?
I know my way around the kitchen."

He looked at her in surprise. "How did
you manage that? I can't imagine the witch
of Wakeford Island allowing anybody in her
private domain."

"I'm a nurse, remember? There are spe-
cial things I have to prepare for your grandfather. She had to show me around."

Dee gestured and he followed her out to
the hall, the two of them tiptoeing quietly
like thieves in the night.

Dee turned on the light in the kitchen,
while Jason took a seat beside the butcher-

block table and followed her movements
with brooding eyes.

Efficiently Dee found a jar of instant coffee, apologizing as she did so. "I don't know
where the regular coffee is," she said, keeping her voice down. "But it's decaffeinated,
so you should be able to sleep." She boiled
some water.

Pulling the remains of the night's roast
from the refrigerator, she unwrapped it and
cut generous slices. Thick slabs of home-
made bread followed, and a small bowl of
butter. She placed all the food before Jason,
then set two mugs of coffee on the table.
Next she put the unneeded things away
neatly, just as she had found them.

Jason had just finished building himself
a huge man-sized sandwich when she sat
down opposite him, taking one of the coffee
mugs for herself.

"This is good," Jason mumbled through a
mouthful of food.

Dee was thinking it was incredible that
a man should have such long eyelashes.
They fringed his dark eyes, almost sweeping
his cheeks when he looked down at his sandwich. The two of them seemed isolated, on
an island within an island, alone in the still
kitchen, with the sleeping house around
them.

"May I ask just what you're doing?" a harsh voice cracked through the stillness, breaking the spell around them.

Dee gave a start, her heart pounding, and turned to see Mrs. Powers glaring at them from the open doorway. The woman was wearing an unattractive plaid robe, tied loosely with a tasseled cord at the shapeless waist. Her hair was down and plaited in a fat pigtail that hung over one shoulder.

Dee laughed nervously. "It seems Jason showed up in the middle of the night and scared me half out of my wits. He was hungry, so I thought I'd fix him a bite before I go back to bed."

Eileen Powers fixed a baleful glare on Jason. "You know how I disapprove of your unannounced comings and goings," she said coldly. "It shows a complete lack of consideration on your part. The house is full of people, and I'd certainly appreciate a little warning when you plan to drop in out of the blue and favor us with your presence."

Jason's voice, when he answered, was ominously low. "Must I remind you again, Mrs. Powers, that this is my home and I'll come and go in it as I please?"

Eileen Powers turned her cold eyes to Dee. "For the moment, I'll ignore Jason's inconsiderate remarks. But I'd like to make something plain to you. I may have to put up with your presence in my kitchen where Mr. Wakeford is concerned, but otherwise, this room is off limits to you. If anyone is to be fed in this household, I will do it. Is that clear?"

"Completely," Dee replied, trying to force back her anger. "I prepared Jason's snack out of consideration for you, so your rest wouldn't be disturbed."

"Don't do me any favors. I know my duty and I do it." She turned sharply to the young man. "I'll take bedding to your old play-room, Jason. Tomorrow I'll turn out another bedroom for Miss Crawford." Her eyes flicked back to Dee. "Now I suggest you get back to bed."

Dee rose slowly, looking at the remains of Jason's midnight snack. "I'd like to straighten up first."

"No. How many times do I have to tell you the kitchen is my responsibility?"

Jason got to his feet. "My bag is in Miss Crawford's room. I'll get it." Brusquely he took Dee's arm and marched her out of the kitchen, closing the door sharply behind him.

Once they were back in the bedroom, Dee looked at Jason in outrage. "Why does Mr.

Wakeford keep her on?" she asked explosively. "That is the rudest woman I have ever seen!"

"But not to old Nick. His every wish is her command. She's been his shadow for thirty years. She manages his house, and she manages his life. Unfortunately, she can't manage me, and that's always been a bone of contention between us."

"Are you often on the island?"

Dee couldn't help asking the question, though she knew she was prying.

"Once I lived here," Jason answered bitterly. "My parents died in an accident when I was nine. I had nowhere else to go. I spent a few years of pure hell here under Eileen Powers's domination. I couldn't wait to escape."

"I can understand that," Dee said softly, feeling a wave of compassion for the young boy who had been trapped in such a circumstance.

A sharp rap at the door announced Eileen Powers. "The couch is made up with fresh sheets," she told Jason stiffly.

Jason pulled the bulging suitcase off the foot of the bed and smiled crookedly. "Thanks for the food, Miss Crawford," he said as he left the room.

This time Dee locked the glass doors before she lay down to sleep. Her mind was in a turmoil, and it seemed sleep would never come. Life seemed to be in a twisted muddle on Wakeford Island. Idly, Dee wondered just how Nicholas Wakeford planned to rewrite his will, then decided it was none of her business. Her only concern should be for her patient's health.

Dee rose early, feeling the effects of her almost sleepless night. Nicholas Wakeford was supposed to receive medication at least forty minutes before he ate his breakfast. She hoped to administer it quietly enough so the old man could get back to sleep before his morning meal actually arrived.

She was surprised to see the door to Nicholas's room swing open just as she reached for the knob. She found herself looking directly into the eyes of Bert Powers.

"What are you doing here?" she asked sharply. "Mr. Wakeford is supposed to be resting!"

The sulky young man glared at her, hatred in his eyes. "What I do is none of your business," he said bitterly. "Why don't you go back where you came from? You're not wanted here! That's what I say."

"What you say is of no importance to me," Dee told him. "The health of my patient is.

In the future, you're to stay out of this room unless he sends for you. Is that clear?"

"You can't give me orders," Bert snarled.

"I just did. I'm going to report this visit to Dr. Winthrop and find out from Mr. Wakeford if you're allowed to come and go from his room whenever you feel like. Now please let me pass."

Dee could feel the anger of Bert as she squeezed past his frame in the doorway. Luckily, the blanketed figure in the bed was still sleeping. What had Bert been doing in his room at this hour?

Setting the medicine tray she was carrying down on the bedside table, Dee touched Nicholas lightly to rouse him and was taken aback when the old man flung out his arms and woke up, flailing at her in confusion. As soon as she had calmed him a bit, she could see the light of reason returning to his eyes.

"You tried to kill me!" he accused.

"You've been having bad dreams," she told him. "Why should I try to kill you?"

Nicholas sat up slowly, putting one hand at the back of his neck, as though it pained him. "Somebody put a pillow over my face," he said. "I couldn't breathe for a while. It was like having a heavy weight on my chest. I blacked out and came back to consciousness to find you leaning over me. What do you expect me to think?"

Dee reached for a glass of water and the little paper cup containing his pills. "Take your medicine, Mr. Wakeford. I'll talk to Dr. Winthrop and have him examine you carefully."

Dutifully Nicholas swallowed his medication. "They all want me dead," he complained. "I'm an old man who's outlived his time."

"That's a lot of nonsense and you know it," Dee said. She straightened his pillows, smoothed the sheet over him, and patted his shoulder. "You try to go back to sleep," she told him. "Dr. Winthrop will be in to see you soon."

Nicholas nodded obediently. His eyes were heavy, and Dee left with the feeling that he would indeed fall asleep again.

Before they sat down to breakfast, Dee called Steve aside and told him about the old man's fears. "I did see Bert leaving his room as I entered," she added. "You don't think there's any possibility—"

Steve shook his head. "No. Bert wanders around the place at will. He's a disagreeable character, but he wouldn't hurt Nicholas. I think Nicholas's experience stemmed from an old man's difficulty in drawing breath, combined with a bad dream. I'll go over and have a look at him, but I'm sure I'll find he's perfectly all right."

Jason did not put in an appearance for breakfast, but Paul was there, again with his briefcase in hand. His eyes traveled over Dee warmly, more warmly than she would have liked.

"I really haven't had time to get better acquainted," Paul told her in an apologetic tone. "I have to spend the morning with old Nick, getting the facts on this new will he's determined to write. Then I'll be working on it all day, I'm sure. At least I'll be back next weekend with the finished product, and as soon as I get his signature, the rest of my time will be free. I'd really like to show you the island personally."

"We'll see," Dee answered. "I really haven't arranged my own free time as yet. Perhaps when you return I'll have my schedule in order."

Steve spent some time right after breakfast with Nicholas, then sent Paul in to conduct his business with the old man. Steve took advantage of that time to take Dee on a short walk about the grounds.

The place was really lovely. Most of the landscaping was natural. Old bent and twisted live oaks were festooned with dripping moss. Magnolias and palms also fought for space in the thick woods, and low-lying palmettos waved their fan-shaped fronds from the edges of the path.

Dee told Steve about Jason's unexpected arrival in the middle of the night, and Steve seemed faintly irritated.

"I'm sorry if he alarmed you," he said. "It's true that Mrs. Powers put you in his room. I was wondering about that at the time. Usually, it's left vacant for Jason, for he's not one to announce his arrivals or departures."

"He seemed honestly concerned about Nicholas," Dee told Steve.

"I'm not surprised," Steve said. "Nicholas has always wanted Jason to take a role in his business concerns, but Jason has always steadfastly refused. Jason is a marine biologist, and his jobs take him to some far-flung corners of the earth. He'll never settle down."

Dee kept stride with Steve's long steps as they turned back toward the house. "From some of the things Jason said, I gathered he must have had an unfortunate childhood here," she told the young doctor.

"He did," Steve said. "There was nobody to look after him but Eileen Powers, and no young companion for him but Bert. Nicholas was away most of the time. The boys took the launch to Galena to attend school when the weather permitted. It wasn't surprising when Jason left for college and seldom returned. With all their fighting, I think he still has a soft spot for the old man."

Looking toward the beach, they saw the object of their discussion jogging rapidly along the surf, moving as though private demons were pursuing him.

Steve looked thoughtful. "In the event that I'm already gone when he sees Nick for the first time, be sure to check on the old man as soon as their talk is over. Seeing his grandson can send Nick's blood pressure skyrocketing."

"I will," Dee said.

Her eyes were fastened on the tall, muscular figure running down the beach. Jason Wakeford was quite an enigma.

CHAPTER FOUR

Dee felt a little strange when the launch left on Sunday morning taking Stephen Winthrop and Paul Kennedy back to the mainland. She had seen little of Jason Wakeford, even less of the distasteful Bert Powers, but too much of the housekeeper, Eileen. The woman continued to be cold and unfriendly, no matter how nice Dee tried to be.

When Bert returned to the island in the afternoon, he brought a canvas bag of mail—left for him at the general store yesterday—most of which he delivered to Nicholas. Dee helped the old man to a comfortable chair by a table in front of his French doors leading to the terrace. The sun shone in brightly, bringing warmth and comfort to Nicholas's old bones.

Dee slit the envelopes for him, knowing

it was difficult for him to do. Then she sat
down unobtrusively and took up a bit of em-
broidery she had brought with her while he
sorted through his mail. An occasional grunt
or chuckle showed Dee that he was absorb-
ing everything he read.

When he had finished, he had the letters
sorted into three neat piles. He indicated
the largest stack, which seemed to be pri-
marily business letters, to Dee and remarked, "Get me a big envelope for these,
and remind me to give them to Paul when
he comes next weekend. He's handling all
my business just now."

"Certainly."

Dee rose and went to get one of the large
envelopes from his desk, where she had seen
them earlier.

As she tucked the letters inside and sealed
the flap, Nicholas took the second stack of
letters and thrust them toward her. "These
are for the wastebasket," he said. "There are
a lot of people out there trying to sell everyone junk!" He snorted. "Life insurance, at
my age. Jogging suits and tennis shoes! Even
ski equipment—in Florida! Not to mention
a sweepstakes for everything under the sun,
including charities. Just dump them all! If
I want to give a donation, I'll give it and not
gamble with it."

Dee smiled wryly as she followed his instructions. She knew exactly what he meant. She got a lot of junk mail herself.

The third stack of letters was the smallest. Nicholas tapped a thick cream-colored envelope with his blunt fingernail. "This is from my grandson, Jason," he said. "He says he's coming to see me. He's my own personal bad penny, you know."

Dee looked at him anxiously, unsure of how to reply.

Nicholas was chuckling to himself. "A lot of spirit, that boy has. Thinks I don't know he's already here. Has been since Friday night sometime. I saw him running on the beach. I know everything that goes on in this house. Tell him to get in here to see me."

"Are you sure you're strong enough?" Dee asked.

"Nonsense. Does me good to see the boy once in a while. I'm going to give him a big surprise this time." Nicholas closed his eyes, seeming almost to doze, but he opened them again. "Yes, sir, a big surprise."

"I'd rather you wait until after your afternoon nap to see him, if you don't mind," Dee said stubbornly.

"If it pleases you." Nicholas reached for

another letter, pushing it toward her pet-ulantly. "I need you to give this to Mrs. Powers, anyway," he said. "A magazine journalist is coming to see me. Her name is Jennifer Lane and she's with *Achievement Magazine*. Wants to interview me, she says."

Dee took the envelope reluctantly. "Does Dr. Winthrop know about this?" she asked.

Nicholas's eyes snapped. "What he doesn't know won't hurt him! I told the Lane woman she could come. Imagine her wanting to write a story about me at my age! It's flattering, young woman, very flattering. She's bringing a photographer with her, too, with the fool name of Gilly Jones. Bert's going to pick them up Thursday."

"I'm not sure you should be subjecting yourself to so much excitement," Dee said, wishing she were able to discuss the situation with Steve.

"I'll see whoever I please, young woman!" Nicholas said querulously. "Now help me to bed for that dratted nap, so I can see my grandson. Round him up and get him in here."

"All right," she reluctantly agreed. "Just as long as you promise not to let him upset you."

Slowly, they crossed the room and Dee helped Nicholas to take off his robe. She sat with him until she was sure he was asleep, then left to look for Eileen Powers with the letter from *Achievement Magazine* in her hand.

Mrs. Powers, amazingly enough, took the news of the two unexpected visitors very well. Apparently, anything Nicholas Wakeford wanted was perfectly all right with Eileen Powers. Breathing a sigh of relief once the housekeeper had been notified, Dee asked her if she knew where Jason might be.

"The last I saw of him, he was headed for the dock to work on his boat," Mrs. Powers answered. "He's a fanatic about that boat. The only free time he has to work on it is when he brings it over here. The rest of the time it just sits in the water at Galena."

Dee thanked her and turned her footsteps toward the dock at the foot of the oyster-shell drive. Jason must have been finishing up, for he was wiping his hands on an oily rag. From the residue of dirt on his T-shirt, it was clear he was working on the engine.

"Can I come aboard?" Dee called lightly.

"Come ahead. Just watch your step."

He gave her a hand as she clambered over

the side, then offered her a seat on a leather cushion.

"Your grandfather wants to see you," Dee said abruptly, "as soon as he wakes from his nap."

"I thought he might." Jason grinned as he sat opposite her, his lean muscles rippling. "I saw him giving me the once-over from his window this morning while I was running on the beach."

"Do you always have to fight with him?" Dee knew she was getting personal, but she was dreading the upcoming confrontation. "He's an old man, Jason. Old and sick. I think you should take that into consideration."

Jason looked at her quizzically. "I don't think you understand us Wakefords. The kind of fighting we do is stimulating. Old Nick thrives on it."

"Well, he's not in any condition to thrive on discord just now," Dee snapped. "I wish you'd remember that when you go in to see him."

Jason seemed amused by her outburst. "I'll be good," he promised. "I have to be. I intend to hit the old man for a loan."

It was Dee's turn to be surprised. "But I thought—"

"You thought we weren't on such good terms, didn't you? I have an opportunity to mount an expedition that could prove profitable to both of us. The old man loves to make a profit. So I'll be good. I promise. Anything else?"

Dee knew he could tell from her face that there was something else on her mind. "Actually, I was wondering about making contact with the mainland. I'd like to call Dr. Winthrop."

He eyed her sharply. "Is it personal, or is there something wrong with old Nick?"

She shook her head. "Not exactly. But he has invited a journalist, Jennifer Lane, and her photographer, Gilly Jones, from *Achievement Magazine* to interview him here on the island. I'm not sure he's up to all that excitement."

Slowly Jason nodded. "I'll brief you on our communication system when we get back to the house. Simple old radio setup. Actually, I'm not surprised they want to interview him. He's accomplished a lot in his day."

"Why don't you two get along? I can tell by what you say that you're basically very fond of him."

Jason laughed. "We're too different, I guess. But don't get me wrong. I do love the old man. However, he's very manipulative, and he has a great respect for the power of money. He's always tried to control me with it, or the lack of it, and could never understand why it isn't as important to me as it is to him."

"Are you his major heir?"

"I don't have the slightest idea. There are some other distant relatives—and then, of course, there's always Eileen and Bert. They can have it as far as I'm concerned. I won't compromise myself for a few bucks."

"Then it doesn't bother you that he's always threatening to change his will?"

"Not really." Jason stood up, stretching. "What really bothers me is that when he starts talking about changing his will, things start happening to him. There's somebody, somewhere, who doesn't want Nicholas playing with that will."

Jason's words were somber, and they brought a chill to Dee's spine. She remembered Bert coming out of Nicholas's room and the old man insisting somebody had tried to smother him while he slept.

Dee saw a smile chase away the shadows on Jason's face as he reached out one sun-warmed hand to her. "Come on back to the house and I'll show you how to make your call," he offered.

As soon as Jason showed her how to do it, Dee understood how simple it was to call the mainland. Steve was on the line in a moment. She could tell by the warmth in his voice that he was glad to hear from her, but he was no happier than she was about the visitors from *Achievement Magazine.*

"I'd really prefer that he didn't have so much excitement right now," he said. "They're arriving on Thursday, you say?"

"According to the letter I read," Dee replied.

"Well, I'll be arriving on Friday afternoon, late. Try to keep them away from Nicholas as much as possible until I can get there. Maybe I can expedite their visit and get them out of there as fast as possible."

"That would be a relief," Dee said.

"Any other problems?" he asked.

"Not really."

"Then I'll see you on Friday." His words were almost a caress, or was she fooling herself? "Maybe we'll have time to get in a bit of swimming on Saturday."

"I'll look forward to it." Dee hung up the phone reluctantly, hating to break her contact with Steve. Somehow things seemed to fall into their proper perspective when he was around.

The week began to pass uneventfully. Dee usually found time in the afternoon to swim while Nicholas napped. She saw very little of Jason, save at mealtimes. Jason seemed true to his word, for his talks with Nicholas had gone surprisingly well.

Jason had taken to visiting with the old man every evening after dinner and sharing a glass of wine and a bit of conversation with him. Dee wondered if Nicholas had agreed to lend Jason the money he asked for, but she didn't have the nerve to ask him. At least there had been no explosion of temper between them.

The evening before the journalist was due to arrive, Dee stepped out on the terrace for a breath of fresh air, only to find Jason there before her. He was standing by the railing, his face highlighted by the moonlight into a profile clean-cut enough to grace a Roman coin.

"Excuse me," Dee said hesitantly. "I didn't mean to interrupt."

He said, "Nonsense. You aren't interrupting anything. Come and join me. I'd enjoy the company."

She moved to the railing and stood beside him, listening to the sounds of the night.

Jason turned toward her. He put out a

hesitant finger and touched her starched cap, pushing it a little awry. "Why are you always wearing that thing?" he asked.

"It's a badge of my profession," Dee said.

"It makes you seem very unapproachable," he said lightly.

"It shouldn't. I'm the same person, in or out of uniform."

"I don't think so." Suddenly, he was very close to her, and there were little lights dancing in his eyes. "I see you in your bathing suit when you go to swim every day. You look so sweet and vulnerable with your hair falling down your back. Then you bunch it up again and hide behind your armor of starch! What's the lady like inside that armor?"

Dee was aware that he was much too close, and she found his nearness disturbing. There was something basic in Jason that appealed to the woman in her. Suddenly, she wished she knew him better, much better.

"We could meet like this more often, spend some time with each other, and perhaps you could find out," she said slowly, surprised to find she was actually flirting with him.

"Why don't we do that?"

His face came closer, and Dee knew he was going to kiss her. She didn't mind. His lips were soft and firm at the same time. She found her arms creeping up about his neck as she returned the kiss with a great deal of pleasure.

When his lips left hers, he didn't let her go at once, but continued to hold her for a few delicious moments.

"I know I shouldn't have done that," he whispered into her hair. "I just gave in to impulse."

"Don't worry about it." Dee smiled gently, pulling away. "It was a nice impulse." She found her hands going to her cap, trying to straighten it where it had slipped to one side.

He grinned crookedly. "Next time don't wear that thing," he said. "How about to-morrow night?"

"Same time, same place," she said lightly and felt him squeeze her hand as he turned to go.

Dee continued to stand on the terrace for a little while, finding herself not at all sleepy. Somehow she hadn't thought of Jason romantically before. Yet she had enjoyed his kiss, wanted him to kiss her, and she was looking forward to meeting him tomorrow night. She smiled to herself as she wondered what Steve would think if he knew she was

kissing her patient's grandson on the terrace! Somehow she knew he wouldn't like
it a bit.

Taking a last look at the moonlit land-
scape, Dee turned to go inside and gave a
frightened gasp as she ran into the figure
of a man who had slipped up behind her
silently. She almost cried out, until she recognized Bert Powers.

"Bert!" she said shakily. "You startled me!
I didn't know you were there."

"I don't suppose you did," he said tone-
lessly. "I saw you out here hugging and kissing Jason. I wonder what Mr. Wakeford
would say if he knew."

"I don't think he would approve of your
spying," Dee retorted. "What I do is none of
your business."

Bert's hand caught her forearm in a bruising grip. "Maybe I'll make it my business,"
he hissed, his eyes narrowing into slits.
"Jason always got the best of everything.
Women fall all over him. Now he's after you,
too."

"Take your hand off my arm," Dee said
sharply. "You're hurting me!"

Slowly he took his hand away, but the
look on his face did not change. "Why don't
you get out of here?" he asked. "Nobody

wants you. Nobody needs you. Now you're going after Jason, like all the others."

"Get out of my way, Bert," Dee ordered. "I'm going inside."

"I'll make you sorry," he said angrily. "I'll make you sorry you ever heard of Wakeford Island!"

Dee swept past him, back into the house, and didn't let her guard down until she was safe in her own bedroom and had locked the doors tightly behind her. Then she found she was trembling. The young man had truly frightened her.

The new bedroom that Mrs. Powers had given her the day after Jason's arrival was as large and well furnished as the one she had slept in the first night she came to the island, but it was on the opposite side of the house from the terrace, so there were no glass doors. Dee found herself thankful. She pulled the shades carefully before she started to get ready for bed.

It seemed she could still feel unfriendly eyes on her, invading her privacy. She hated the feeling, but it persisted even after she had turned out the light and pulled the thin covers over her.

CHAPTER FIVE

Jason arranged to have breakfast with Dee the next morning, and his manner was warm and friendly, even tinged with flirtation. She became increasingly aware of what an attractive man he was, once the angry scowl had left his face and was replaced by a smile. Being in a confiding mood, she mentioned her encounters with Bert, playing down the possible "smothering" incident as Steve had done. Jason said nothing, but he listened carefully.

Dee happened to be doing exercises with Nicholas later when the launch came in bringing Jennifer Lane and her photographer. Bert had driven them up from the landing in his jeep, and there was a real flurry of activity as the bags were unloaded.

There was no way Dee could mistake which one of the young women below was Jennifer Lane—for Gilly Jones was laboring under a load of cameras and other equipment. Gilly was a green-eyed redhead, with her hair bobbed short. Jennifer, on the other hand, had the body of a model and moved with fluid grace. A mane of straight straw-colored hair was pulled back from her face with tortoise-shell barrettes and fell like a cascade of shining water down her back.

From what Dee could see from the old man's window, Jennifer was giving orders imperiously, running Gilly ragged, until they finally disappeared from view.

Dee turned from the window to confront Nicholas. "Your magazine people are here," she said.

"Already?" A scowl crossed his face.

"You shouldn't invite people if you don't want them," Dee chided. "They'll be wanting to see you as soon as they're settled."

"Well, I'm not ready to see them!" Nicholas creased his craggy face as he reached into his bathrobe pocket and pulled out a thin bunch of keys. "The Lane woman wanted access to my files. This is the key to my study. Mrs. Powers can show you where it is. The other keys open file drawers." Carefully he removed one key from the ring. "Except for this one, and that's a private file. There ought to be enough material in the others to keep them busy."

"This won't satisfy her for long," Dee warned him. "She's going to insist on talking to you."

"I won't talk until I'm ready," he flared. "And I'll choose the time, not you or Miss Lane. Now help me into my bed. I'm tired and in no mood to talk to reporters."

"All right," Dee said patiently. "Then up with you. It's still rather early for your nap."

"Not if I'm tired."

Nicholas kept muttering under his breath as she helped him across the room. He continued to grumble until she had him settled for his nap. Then he closed his eyes much too easily, and Dee felt sure he was faking. Nevertheless, she went toward the kitchen, putting the ring of keys carefully in her uniform pocket. She found Eileen Powers busily beating the batter for a spice cake. The smell of the spices was mouth-watering.

"Mr. Wakeford doesn't want to talk to the reporter today," Dee told her. "He suggested we let Miss Lane and her assistant into his study to go through his files. I understand you can show me just where it is."

Eileen gave a particularly vicious swipe
with her wooden spoon. "No good will come
of it," she said harshly. "It's a mistake to let
other people nose around in your business.
Did he give you the keys?"

"He did." Dee dangled them before her.
"All except the one to his private files."

"Well, I'm glad he has a little sense left.
I'll show you the study, and you'll find the
Lane woman and her friend having a little
tea party with Jason on the terrace."

Dee followed Eileen to a door, tucked away
unobtrusively behind the attic stairs. The
housekeeper then left without a word. Dee
slipped the key into the lock and opened the
door, prepared to do a little cleaning if it
were necessary before she turned the room
over to Jennifer and Gilly.

Surprisingly, it was neat and orderly.
Thick   leather-bound   books   filled   the
ceiling-high shelves behind the old oak desk,
and the remainder of the room was filled
with the memorabilia of a successful man.
In a silver frame on his desk, Dee saw the
photograph of a much younger Nicholas with
a lovely woman wearing old-fashioned at-
tire and a little boy dressed in a sailor suit.
That must have been Jason's father, Dee
surmised.

Nicholas had been a handsome man in his youth, with a remarkable resemblance to his grandson.

Around the room were many photographs of Nicholas, taken with various people of note over the past few decades. It was a shrine to the old man, and Dee hoped Jennifer Lane would do nothing to desecrate it.

Closing the door gently behind her, she headed toward the terrace. It was easy to find the little group, for the sound of conversation and light laughter drifted into the house through the open doors.

Jennifer was smiling into Jason's face, while he hovered much too closely above her chair. Dee felt an unaccustomed stab of jealousy as she saw his dark head bent so closely over the light one.

Jason looked up at the sound of her footsteps, and a crooked smile lighted his face. "Oh, Dee! There you are!"

Dee returned the smile but tried to keep it impersonal. She caught Jennifer's gray eyes in a direct gaze. "I take it you're Jennifer Lane."

"Right." The gray eyes looked her over coolly. "And this is my assistant, Gilly Jones."

Gilly bobbed her head as Dee nodded in recognition. "I'm Dee Crawford, Mr. Wakeford's private nurse. I'm afraid he's having one of his off days. He suggested I take you to his study and give you access to his files, so you can get your background information before the actual interview."

Jennifer's eyes narrowed. "Then Wakeford is really a sick man?"

Dee shook her head. "Not seriously. He's recuperating well. He's just a little tired today, and I feel it would be better to delay the interview until his doctor arrives tomorrow evening."

"Well, I hope there's enough material to keep us busy until then. My time is valuable, too, Miss Crawford."

"I'm sure you'll find everything you need. Just indicate when you're ready, and I'll take you to the study." Dee could be every bit as businesslike as Jennifer Lane.

Jason leapt to attention and pulled out a chair for Dee. "Meanwhile, why don't you join us in a glass of iced tea?" As soon as she was seated, he reached for the tongs, dropped some ice in a tall glass, filled it with the amber fluid, then topped it with a sprig of mint.

Dee took it gratefully and relaxed against

the back of her chair, the glass resting on the white wrought-iron table before her. She sat quietly, satisfied to observe. She noticed that Jennifer was still nagging Gilly, ordering her to take shots of this and that, seemingly at random, but often enough so that the girl had no chance to sit still and relax. It occurred to Dee that so far she hadn't heard Gilly utter a word. She wondered if the poor girl could talk.

Jennifer certainly could. She kept up a sprightly conversation with Jason, asking him questions now and then. Dee found herself wanting to warn him to be careful of what he said, for the journalist's questions were somewhat tricky.

Jennifer seemed to be aware that there was a rift between Jason and the old man. Obviously, she had done her homework on the Wakefords. Happily, Dee soon found that Jason could handle himself very well and had no need of her warning.

Finally, Jennifer must have felt her well of information had run dry, for she turned to Dee with a shrug and asked to be escorted to the study. As Dee rose from her chair, she noticed Jennifer motioning to Gilly imperiously.

The two young women followed Dee, and she soon had them involved with the files, with Gilly dutifully taking notes for Jennifer.

The two women spent the remainder of that afternoon in the study. Dee passed the door a few times during the day, only to see the pair going through the files feverishly, pulling out folders to add to the stack on the desk. The last time she passed, she saw Jason had joined them. Her back stiffened, and she continued without acknowledging any of them. It was Jason's own business if he preferred their company to hers!

Dee felt like a fifth wheel at dinner, for Jennifer continued to monopolize the conversation, asking Jason for more and more details about the old man's life. When Dee finally rose and quietly left the table, she didn't believe any of the others was aware that she was gone. She felt distinctly out of sorts as she went to prepare her patient— who had eaten earlier—for bed.

Dee found Nicholas crusty and temperamental, but his general physical condition seemed to be excellent.

"What is that woman doing in my study?" he asked.

"Just what you suggested," Dee retorted. "Going through your files."

"I may have made a mistake, asking her here," he said, sighing.

"You'll never know until you talk with her," Dee answered.

"Make 'em wait, I always say," the old man said smugly. "Puts 'em on edge every time and gives me a distinct advantage."

"You never miss a trick, do you?" Dee sat down on the bed, looking at the old man fondly.

"You're pretty sharp yourself," Nicholas responded. "How are you getting along with my grandson?"

Dee had the grace to blush, and she turned away, hoping Nicholas hadn't seen the telltale flush on her cheeks. "He seems like a nice enough young man," she answered uneasily.

"Nice enough?" Nicholas gave a snort. "There's something going on between you. Nice enough, indeed!"

Dee stood up, smoothing her skirt. "You're an exasperating man, Nicholas Wakeford."

"And you're an attractive young woman. Jason isn't blind, you know." Nicholas eyed her keenly.

"No, he isn't. He seems quite taken with Jennifer Lane, as a matter of fact," Dee replied a little sharply.

"Aha! The green demon of jealousy rears its ugly head!" Nicholas chuckled. "You can't fool me!"

Dee lifted her chin defiantly. "Stop teasing me. I'm here as your nurse and nothing else. Now turn over and I'll give you a back rub. This conversation has gone on long enough."

Dee gave him a vigorous massage and left him propped up in bed, leaning against plump pillows, a fat book on his lap.

As she entered her own bedroom, she heard a rap on Nicholas's door and knew Jason had come to see his grandfather for his nightly visit.

She slipped out of her uniform and indulged in a long, cool shower. Leaving her hair down, she donned a sundress of poppy-red cotton and thrust her feet into matching sandals, then started for the terrace before she could change her mind. After all, Jason had said he would meet her there tonight.

As she approached the living-room doors leading out to the terrace, she slowed her footsteps and found herself glad the room was dark so she couldn't be seen, for outside, standing almost where she and Jason had stood the night before, was Jennifer. She was right beside Jason, engaged in a low, murmuring conversation that was too faint for Dee to understand.

Dee beat a hasty retreat, hating herself

for having shown up there at all. Jason was an incorrigible flirt. Apparently, any woman would do, any woman at all.

Dee tried to read herself to sleep, but instead found herself pacing the floor. What was the matter with her? She wasn't romantically involved with Jason Wakeford! What did it matter where he was or who he was with?

Her sleep was restless and interrupted by dreams, none of which she could remember on waking. She felt logy, with the beginning of a headache, and knew she would pay for her almost sleepless night.

A cold shower gave her back some of her vitality. She donned her uniform and slipped out to give Nicholas his morning medication. He was grumbling and irritable.

"I don't know why you can't just leave the pills here and let me sleep," he fussed.

"If you want to eat on time, you'll take your medication on time," she threatened him, and he took it at last like a sulky child.

Jason seemed to be eyeing her curiously at the breakfast table, but Dee tried to avoid his gaze. Jennifer, sleek and stunning in an ice-blue cotton dress, kept him involved in a steady stream of conversation. Once breakfast was over, Jennifer insisted Jason return with her and Gilly to the study. Dee took Nicholas his breakfast.

She managed to stay closeted away with her patient for most of the morning, helping him with his exercises and reading to him from one of his favorite books. She was ready for a break by the time she settled him down for his afternoon nap.

Going directly to her bedroom, she reached for her sleek yellow swimsuit. Loosening her hair from its confining bun, she felt free and easy. As she grabbed for a towel and made her way to the sandy beach, she didn't admit, even for a moment, that she hoped Jason might join her there.

She noticed Bert heading out to sea in the launch and realized he must be going for Steve and Paul. What a relief it would be to have them back again!

Dee spread out her oversized bath towel and, sitting on it, began to apply suntan lotion to her shoulders and arms. She felt a shadow move over her and knew without looking up that it was Jason.

"Why have you been avoiding me, young lady?"

Dee slowed the rubbing motion of her hand. "You seemed to be busy enough with our journalist friend."

He lowered himself to the sand beside her, and she noticed he was wearing cutoff jeans, which gave him a boyish appeal. "Sometimes it pays to be friendly," he retorted. "You find out some interesting things that way."

Dee's arm stilled, and she stopped applying the lotion long enough to ask, "What kind of interesting things?"

He picked up a handful of sand and let it sift through his fingers. "Jennifer has come up with an old letter that indicates my grandfather was once involved with Eileen Powers."

Dee gasped. "Involved? How?"

"The letter mentioned a wedding. Unfortunately, there's no date and the envelope is missing."

"Then you saw the letter?"

"Jennifer showed it to me, yes." Jason dusted his hands off, then wiped them on his lean thighs.

"Come on, Jason, give. What did the letter say?"

"It was from Eileen to Nicholas, giving him the time for the wedding and begging him not to be late—saying it was the beginning of a whole new life for them both."

"I don't believe it," Dee said positively.

"There's some other explanation."

"Jennifer believes it," Jason said. "She plans to ask Nicholas if Bert is his son."

Dee shook her head incredulously. "That has to be impossible. Nicholas isn't the kind of man to deny his own flesh and blood."

"Stranger things have happened," Jason said calmly.

Dee was outraged. "You don't believe that preposterous story, do you? Why, that would make Bert your—your—"

"Half uncle," Jason supplied placidly. "And, no, I don't believe it. If Eileen Powers had that kind of a hold over Nicholas, I think the world would know it, and she certainly wouldn't be working as the Wakeford housekeeper."

"Still, there's something between her and Nicholas," Dee mused thoughtfully. "I just don't think he would keep her on if there weren't."

"I guess we'll just have to wait and see what Nick has to say to Jennifer," Jason said quietly.

"He'll be furious," Dee replied.

"Perhaps. It'll make for an interesting interview, anyway." The serious look on his face was replaced by a crooked grin. "Enough about Eileen and Bert. I'd rather talk about you. Nicholas has been hinting that there's something between you and Winthrop. Is that true?"

Dee shook her head. "I only met Dr. Winthrop when I agreed to take this job."

"Well, I've never taken another guy's girl, but I'm giving you fair warning. This may be an exception."

Dee's smile softened her words. "That remains to be seen," she told him. "Jason, I don't know a thing about you. We've had no time to become decently acquainted. You're a very attractive man, but we've never talked about anything but Nicholas."

He opened his hands innocently. "Here I am. What do you want to know?"

"What do you do for a living?"

"I'm a marine biologist, as you may have heard. And I do a little honest piracy on the side. When I discover a bonanza in the shape of a sunken ship, I set up a salvage party. I've made some real finds that way."

"And Nicholas doesn't like what you do?" Dee quirked an eyebrow at him.

"Oh, it's not what I do, but what I don't do. He wants me on the board of directors of some of his widespread companies, playing puppet to the pull of his strings. I can't do that. I enjoy my freedom too much. The lure of the open sea, the feel of a good ship under my feet—no, I wasn't made for boardrooms and dry, dusty stock reports." He smiled ruefully.

"What if it's true, Jason? What if there was some secret marriage? What if Bert is Nicholas's son? What would that mean to you?"

"It would hurt because it would mean Nicholas had lied to me all these years," he admitted. "It would also be painful to think I was related to such a jerk."

"But could that be the reason Eileen thinks Bert should share in Nicholas's will?" Dee asked. "Could it be that Bert really did try to smother the old man to keep him from changing that will?"

"I don't know," Jason answered gravely. "I just don't know. I don't like the way things are shaping up, either, and that's why I'm hanging around to keep an eye on Nick. I guess we'll know the truth eventually. Meanwhile, let's go for a swim!"

Laughing, he pulled her to her feet and they ran together to the water where the waves foamed like sea lace and the green depths were soft and warm.

CHAPTER SIX

Dee didn't realize how much she had missed Steve until she saw his tall figure walking up to the house from the landing. He had removed his suit coat and was holding it over one shoulder.

Dee didn't try to hide her delight at seeing him. She rushed outside and stood waiting for him, a beaming smile on her face.

He reached for her hands, and for a moment she thought he meant to kiss her, but he merely regarded her warmly and asked how the week had gone.

"Well enough," she assured him. "There are some things we should talk about, but we can do it later."

Over his shoulder she saw Bert driving the jeep up the road with Paul Kennedy as his only passenger. Obviously, Paul preferred riding to walking.

The attorney dismounted when the jeep reached them. He was carrying his trusty briefcase, as usual, and he, too, clasped Dee's hand in greeting. "Just as pretty as ever, I see," he said expansively.

She didn't reply. She merely smiled and escorted the men inside.

"Was it hot on the mainland?" she asked as she opened the door.

"Scorching," Paul answered. "It's good to get away for the weekend. There's always a nice breeze out here." He tapped his briefcase. "Nicholas's work is all done, and all I require is his signature and those of a couple of witnesses." He winked at Dee and gave her arm a little squeeze. "That gives us time to get better acquainted."

It didn't take the men long to freshen up for dinner. Dee was still in her uniform, since she knew she would be attending Nicholas later in the company of Dr. Winthrop, but she noticed Jennifer had really dressed up for the occasion. She wore a silky white designer outfit that showed off her tan to perfection and a lovely strand of pearls.

Gilly was wearing a simple blue cotton dress. She immediately took a seat away from the others, unobtrusive as always.

Dee sat near the quiet photographer, determined to talk to her. Jennifer was in her glory, with two new men to enchant. Jason merely ate and observed, and the only time Dee saw a flicker of interest on his face was when their eyes met across the table.

"Tell me, Gilly," Dee said, balancing a pink curly shrimp on her fork, "what do you think of the island?"

Gilly looked at Dee, eyes wide, as though she couldn't believe she was being addressed directly. "It's all right, I guess," she said hesitantly.

"Have you been with *Achievement Magazine* very long?" Dee was determined to keep the conversation going.

"About two years." Gilly looked desperate, as though wishing someone would come and rescue her.

Dee realized suddenly that the girl was painfully shy. Gilly's face was flushed a dull red from the unaccustomed attention, a color that did nothing to enhance her red hair.

"Do you enjoy your work?" Dee persisted.

"Yes, I guess so." Gilly looked down into her lap where she was twisting her napkin nervously.

"I understand from Jason that you and

Jennifer have made some interesting dis-
coveries in Mr. Wakeford's old files," Dee
said.

"I—I really wouldn't know about that."
Gilly looked so miserable that Dee finally
decided to have mercy on her.

"While you're here, I'll be happy to show
you around the island," she told Gilly. "You
should take a little time off to enjoy yourself. All work and no play makes Jill a dull
girl, you know."

Gilly looked stricken, and her face colored
even more. Dee could have cut out her
tongue. Did Gilly think she was accusing
her of being dull? She hoped not. She hadn't
meant it that way at all.

It was a relief to almost everyone when
dinner was finally over and they could go
their separate ways. Steve wanted to see his
patient, so Dee went with him to Nicholas's
quarters, leaving Jennifer and Gilly with
Paul and Jason.

After his examination, Steve beamed at
Nicholas. "You seem to be in the pink of
condition. Looks like Dee has been good for
you."

"She's stubborn," Nicholas said. "Tough
and stubborn."

"It takes one to know one," Dee murmured.

Nicholas peered at her through his bushy brows. "See?" he said quickly. "Mouthy, too."

Steve pulled up a straight chair and sat down. "Now what's all this about your inviting a reporter here? You really shouldn't have done that."

"I have the right to see anybody I choose," Nick insisted stubbornly.

"I'm not arguing that point. However, I feel you should have your interview with them tomorrow, while I'm here to step in if things get out of hand," Steve said seriously.

"Is Kennedy here, too?" Nicholas asked fretfully. "I want to take care of my will tomorrow."

"You can do that, too. Meanwhile, I'll inform Miss Lane that you'll talk with her tomorrow. Incidentally, I still insist on being present. With Dee. Do you have any difficulty with that?" Steve asked bluntly.

"No," Nicholas answered. "Just don't butt in unless it's necessary."

"Agreed. I'd simply like to have the matter over and behind us." He stood, seeming very tall as he towered over the bed. "I brought a wheelchair over on the launch. I think it's time you went for some little excursions and got some fresh air."

"Good!" Dee's eyes sparkled. "That should

give him an incentive to gain strength."

Nicholas waved a hand at her impatiently. "Stop talking about me as though I weren't here," he ordered imperiously.

"I wasn't talking to you," Dee retorted.

Steve turned his attention to Nicholas. "How have you been sleeping?" he asked.

"All right, for the last few nights. Nobody's tried to smother me since last weekend," the old man replied stoutly.

"That was your imagination and you know it," Steve answered patiently.

"I suppose you think I'm too old and senile to know when I have a pillow pressed over my face," Nick said.

"Keep up the sleeping pills and his morning medication," Steve said to Dee, ignoring Nick's outburst. "I think we can dispense with the noon prescription."

"Good." Dee wrote herself a note and slipped it into her pocket. Walking over to the desk, she took the silver cover off Nick's dinner plate and looked it over carefully. "He's eating well," she observed to Steve. "And he's been having a nightly glass of wine with Jason."

Steve raised an eyebrow. "So you're not feuding with the young man just now?"

Nicholas looked like a thundercloud. "I

don't feud with my grandson, as you so eloquently put it," he snapped. "He came up with a good business proposition and we're discussing it. It's as simple as that."

"I didn't think things were ever simple where you and Jason are concerned," Steve told him boldly. "Remember when you told me to keep him away from you at all costs?"

"That was months ago," Nicholas answered, nettled. "Things change."

"Well, it seems they've changed for the better for you, and I'm happy to see it. I'll talk to you again tomorrow."

Nicholas sighed heavily. "I suppose it's inevitable."

Dee knew she needed to talk to Steve in private, but it seemed the very walls had ears with all the people who were currently living in the house on Wakeford Island. Finally, she remembered Nicholas's study and took Steve there, carefully closing the door behind them.

"What's troubling you, Dee?" Steve sat down in a brown leather chair, sinking back comfortably as she did the same in a facing chair.

"Frankly, Steve, I'm not sure. You know how, in our work, sometimes you have to proceed on instinct alone. I just have a very strong feeling that something is not right somewhere."

"Are you talking about Nicholas's health, or something else?"

"I suppose something else. Nicholas's health seems to be improving every day," she admitted.

Steve leaned forward. "You've been on my mind all week," he said. "What do you think of Nicholas himself?"

"I get fonder of him every day," Dee answered truthfully. "I've found I have little trouble with him if I approach him on his own level. He likes to intimidate people, but basically he's as tame as a teddy bear."

"I've heard Nick called a lot of things, but never a teddy bear," Steve chuckled. "It looks like I came up with the right girl for the job."

Dee asked, "Have you any idea what's in the will that Nicholas is so determined to change? I get the feeling there are some people around who don't want that will changed."

Steve shook his head. "No, I don't. Nick is very reticent about his private affairs."

Dee gave the doctor a troubled look. "Jennifer Lane claims to have come across some correspondence that indicates Nick may once have been married to Eileen Powers."

Steve looked concerned. "And she plans to confront Nicholas with that?"

Dee nodded. "Apparently."

"Then I'm glad I insisted on being present. Nick won't like it. Not at all. He worshipped Jason's grandmother. Her name was Gwyndolyn, and he refuses to talk about her to this day. He would consider talk of a second marriage tantamount to a betrayal of Gwyn's memory." Abruptly he stopped talking and got to his feet. "Sometime, when I have a chance, maybe I'll take you for a nice long walk across the island. It'll do you good to get away for an hour or so. Anyway, we'll talk again when we know more about Jennifer's story."

Dee smiled. "It's a date."

Together they strolled out to the terrace, where Paul sat with the two young women. Jason was conspicuous by his absence. Dee surmised that he was visiting his grandfather. Paul seemed more than delighted with their return, though he was being his charming self to Jennifer and Gilly.

Paul made his way to Dee's side immediately, put a cold drink in her hand, and steered her toward the railing out of earshot of the others.

"Did you miss me?" he asked outrageously.

"Don't be silly, Paul. I don't know you well enough to miss you."

"Then that's a situation we'll have to rectify."

Dee indicated the women behind her. "There's a whole terraceful of attractive ladies out here. Why pick on me?"

"Because you can't improve on perfection!" He winked at her intimately. "As long as we're both going to be together often on the island, we might as well be friends."

Dee smiled at him. "Why not?" she asked lightly.

Even after Jason came back from his grandfather's room, Dee had no chance to speak to him alone. She joined in the general conversation, but her heart wasn't in it. The gathering on the terrace could have been any group of young people socializing —instead of several individuals brought together by the pressure of circumstances.

Dee had been telling the truth when she said she was growing increasingly fond of Nicholas Wakeford. There seemed to be a bond of understanding between her and the old man, and she wanted to see him enjoy his last years in good health.

Her eyes wandered from one young man to another. For a girl with no romantic entanglements, she was suddenly inundated with possibilities. She knew Steve Winthrop was attracted to her, as she was to him. Paul Kennedy she wasn't sure of. He came on strong to every woman he met, but he certainly seemed to like her. And there was Jason. Jason Wakeford, with the curling dark hair and eyes that changed from moody to merry on whim.

An interesting situation was shaping up, but there were many unknown factors. Jennifer Lane was a potential threat. She was glamorous and had an interesting occupation. Wasn't she more intriguing than a mere nurse? Well, at least she would be gone soon.

When Dee went to Nicholas's room for a bedtime checkup, she found him peacefully asleep, but she still couldn't shake the feeling of foreboding that had been with her all day.

She went to bed secure in the knowledge that Steve was under the same roof, sharing the responsibility. If any emergency arose, he could handle it.

The next day dawned cloudless and bright. Dee got up early to give Nicholas his first medication and then made herself a cup of instant coffee and went out on the terrace to watch the morning sun. The world looked new-washed, and the day was so still she could hear the waves as they lapped at the shore.

"You're up and about early."

Dee gave an involuntary start, not expecting to hear a voice so early in the morning. Looking about her, she spied Jason approaching from the direction of the garden.

"Look who's talking!" she said. "You're a bit early yourself, aren't you?"

He stepped up to the terrace and straddled the chair opposite her. "I've been keeping an eye on the old man's room. You made me a little nervous with your talk of pillows over the face and strange things happening."

"Oh, Jason! Steve thinks that was his imagination. Haven't you had any sleep at all?" she asked, distressed.

"I can nap a bit this morning now that you're up and watching. Winthrop's around to keep an eye on things, too," he said. "Nick told me you plan to be present during Jennifer's interview."

"Yes, we do." Dee nodded. "I'm not sure

Jennifer can be trusted not to upset him."

"If she goes through with her present plans, she'll upset him plenty," Jason assured her.

"By the way," Dee asked curiously, "did you ever know Bert's father?"

Jason looked thoughtful. "As a matter of fact, I didn't," he replied. "I tried to steer the conversation that way last night when I was with Nick. All I could learn was that his name was Calvin Powers, and he was killed in an accident."

"Didn't you say your parents also died in an accident?" Dee asked, speculation in her voice.

"My parents went down together in an airline disaster," Jason said. "But that was a few years later."

"Then there couldn't have been a connection," Dee sighed.

"No. And Eileen Powers has been here as long as I can remember," Jason said.

"Was she here acting as housekeeper while your grandmother was alive?" Dee persisted.

Jason looked amused. "She may seem ancient, but I don't think she's quite that old. My grandmother's name was Gwyndolyn. Nick always calls her Gwyn whenever he talks about her, which is seldom. She was lost at sea when my father, Alex, was rather young. Dad remembered her vaguely—said she was a beautiful woman. Right after her death, Nicholas bought the island and became a recluse."

"Then Eileen raised your father as well?"

"Not exactly. Dad was a grown man before she came here—but he didn't like her any better than I do." Jason reached for Dee's cup and brazenly took a sip from it. "Hey, that's good!" he exclaimed.

"I'll get you some." Dee tried to rise, but Jason held her down with a hand on her shoulder.

"Never mind. I'll get my own on my way to bed."

Dee looked at him, her eyes melting. "I feel better knowing you're keeping an eye on things," she confessed.

Jason looked suddenly grim. "Nobody's getting into Nick's room again without my seeing him—and that goes double for Bert Powers."

Dee glanced at him over her cup. "He's been keeping a very low profile," she remarked.

"I don't think he's very sociable," Jason said wryly.

Dee gazed directly into Jason's eyes, holding them with her own. "Jason, please tell me—has Nick mentioned what he's doing with his will?"

Jason shook his head firmly. "I had a copy of the old one. He had left the house, the island, and a large bequest to Eileen and Bert. A lot went to charities, and Paul had set up a trust to take care of the island for the Powers family."

"And you?" she asked bluntly.

He chuckled. "He was angry with me at the time. He cut me off with five thousand dollars and some sharp words."

"And that doesn't bother you?" Dee asked in outrage.

"Really, it doesn't." Suddenly, he leaned over and brushed her lips with his—a soft, quick caress. "It bothers me more wondering how he's changed it this time." He sighed. "I'll see you later," he murmured, "when we've seen the last of *Achievement Magazine.*"

Dee watched his lithe form as it disappeared into the darkness of the house. There was a stubborn tilt to her chin. She meant to find out just what Nicholas was doing with his will that was causing so much unrest. The only person who knew for sure was

Paul Kennedy, and Dee intended to haunt his footsteps until she could force him to tell her something, anything, to help allay her suspicions.

Eileen's presence on the island was still an enigma. Dee refused to believe for a moment that she had ever had a romantic involvement with Nicholas. It was simply preposterous. But why was she here, and what was the mysterious power she wielded over the old man?

It was early afternoon before Nick sent for Jennifer. Dee alerted Steven, and they went to Nick's room together for the promised interview, to find Jennifer and Gilly already there. Nick was in his new wheelchair, with a brightly colored afghan over his bony knees. Jennifer sat in a straight chair beside him, trying to handle her pad and pen and tape recorder as unobtrusively as possible.

Jennifer gave them a cold glance. "I'm not sure we need an audience for this interview," she said resentfully.

"Sorry," Steve answered cheerfully, sitting himself down squarely beside Nicholas. "Without us, there won't be any interview."

The furious reporter gave a flip twist of her head and turned her attention back to

Nicholas. "We've done our research well. I have a complete list of the charities you've funded, and the firms you've been involved with. What I'd like to get now are the real facts about the man himself. You've been practically a recluse for many years. Since your first wife died, as a matter of fact. To what do you attribute this?"

"And why do you refer to Gwyn as my first wife? She's my only wife!" Nick fastened his keen eyes upon her. "I discuss Gwyn with no one. No one, do you understand?"

"But—" The young reporter turned in annoyance as she was interrupted by a rap on the door.

Paul Kennedy entered and began to apologize immediately. "I didn't know you were busy," he said softly. "I brought the will for you to sign, but I can come back later."

Nick wheeled his chair around. "Now will do just fine. We even have the people here to witness it for us."

As Paul came into the room with his ever-present briefcase, Jennifer snapped, "I wasn't aware I would have to conduct an interview in the middle of homecoming week!"

"It's hardly that." Steve relinquished his

chair to Paul and slid a little tray table between Kennedy and Nicholas.

"This won't take long," Paul said. He
opened the briefcase, took out the legal-
looking document in its blue backing, and
turned the pages rapidly until he found the
last one. "I'll need your signature right
here," he pointed out to Nicholas, "and two
witnesses here, and here, after which each
page should be initialed."

Nicholas scrawled his signature, a thick
black almost indecipherable scribble, and
offered the pen to Jennifer. "Maybe you two
ladies will do the honors?"

Jennifer shrugged. "Why not?" She af-
fixed her own signature, then gave the pen
to Gilly. "Do I get to read the contents? I
don't like signing something I haven't read."

"Maybe later." Nicholas folded up the will,
then gave it directly to Paul. "Don't leave
this lying around," he ordered. "Keep it on
your person until you're back on the mainland and can get me a copy for myself."

Paul nodded and thrust it into the inside
pocket of his suit jacket before he resnapped
his briefcase and rose to take his departure.

"Sorry for the inconvenience," he said as
he closed the door behind him.

"This is very interesting," Jennifer said

softly. "So you're changing your will!"

"Obviously."

"In favor of Eileen Powers, perhaps?" The reporter's eyes glittered.

Nicholas gave her an honest look of amazement. "What?" he asked.

"I'm interested in your relationship with Eileen Powers," Jennifer said. "I understand there was once a romantic relationship between you."

Dee held her breath. She could almost feel the icy rage building in Nicholas. He glared at Jennifer coldly from flashing eyes half hidden beneath his craggy brows. "Your impertinence is only equaled by your rudeness, young woman!"

Jennifer smiled arrogantly, pushing ahead. "Our readers are interested in the total man, Mr. Wakeford. His loves and hates, likes and dislikes—"

"Let's just say I owe Mrs. Powers a deep debt of gratitude," Nicholas conceded gruffly.

"But why?" Jennifer was adamant.

"Frankly, that's none of your business!" Nicholas was staring at Jennifer as though she were a bit of vermin.

"Isn't it true that Bert Powers is your son? That you have disinherited your own grandson, Jason, in his favor, and that's what this will-signing is all about?" Jennifer asked.

"This interview is over!" Nick roared. "Get her out of here, Winthrop!"

Steve was on his feet instantly. "It would be best if you left now," he told Jennifer. Putting his hand on her arm, he tried to guide her toward the door.

Gilly was already there, looking scared, her cameras bobbing about her neck like oversized pendants.

"I have ways of getting to the truth," Jennifer threatened. "It would be better if I learned the truth from you, believe me!"

"If you publish one untrue word about me, you'll learn firsthand about the laws of libel," Nicholas said. "Now get out of here."

"You'll be sorry," Jennifer called over one shoulder as Steve forced her and a nervous Gilly out into the hallway, locking the door behind them.

Dee was already hovering over Nicholas, taking his pulse, which was pounding. His face was white and pinched, the anger that was evident in every line of his body taking possession of him, tearing him apart.

Steve had taken a portable blood-pressure unit from his bag and was busy wrapping the cuff about the old man's skinny arm.

"It was a mistake," Nick groaned between clenched teeth. "I should never have invited that woman here. To cast slurs on my love for Gwyn—to even suggest I would look at another woman—"

"Shh!" Dee tried to calm him as she prepared the sedative injection Steve ordered.

As soon as it was administered, Dee could feel the tension slowly leaving the old man's body.

"You'll sleep a while now and wake up feeling fit as a fiddle," Steve promised.

"Get that Lane woman out of here," Nick ordered. "I never want to see her face again."

After they succeeded in getting Nick into bed, Steve and Dee paused in the hall outside his room for a whispered consultation.

"It seems our inquiring reporter didn't learn a thing," Steve said.

"Neither did we," Dee said. "I wish I knew what was in that will. All the trouble seems to stem from that."

"Paul seems quite taken with you," Steve said slyly. "Do you think you might wheedle the information out of him?"

Dee winced. "Wheedle? That's a poor choice of words. I wonder if it's unethical to divulge the contents of a will."

Steve looked a little embarrassed. "It probably is," he admitted. "It's a confidence between lawyer and client, similar to doctor-patient relationships. However, you might be able to find out what's *not* in the will."

Dee sighed. "All right. I'll try. Meanwhile, we have to usher Miss Lane off the island diplomatically."

"I think she'll be ready to go after that taste of old Nick's temper," Steve said.

They were wrong. Jennifer was furious at Nick's treatment of her and refused to budge.

"I will not leave this island until I get the full interview I was promised," she said stormily when Dee entered the room she shared with Gilly.

For the first time, Gilly spoke up on her own behalf. "I really think we should go, Jennifer," she said. "I don't think Mr. Wakeford is going to talk to us again."

"Oh, yes, he will!" Jennifer retorted.

"I'm afraid Gilly is right," Dee broke in softly. "He's really a very stubborn man. Furthermore, he's not well, and having you here upsets him. I'm afraid you'll have to go back on the launch tomorrow with Bert."

"We'll see. First, I intend to talk to Mrs. Powers and her son, Bert—and perhaps Jason Wakeford, as well."

"Then I would arrange those interviews in a hurry, Miss Lane, because when the launch leaves, we expect you to be on it."

Jennifer gave Dee a scathing look. "I'm not sure why you think you have the authority to order me around," she answered.

"We'll see what Jason has to say about this."

"Do that." Dee turned her back squarely on the reporter and marched out of the room.

Arranging a meeting with Paul was as easy as Dee had expected it to be. Since there was nowhere in the house they could talk for any length of time free from interruption, Dee arranged to meet him down by the wharf at ten that evening, after dinner was over and she had made her nightly visit to Nicholas.

Dee thought she detected a satisfied smirk on Paul's face, and she hated herself for letting him think it was his many charms that had led her to make the evening tryst with him. However, she told herself, it was all in a good cause.

The first opportunity she had to speak to Jason was during her afternoon swim, when he showed up casually, as though it were expected.

Dee briefed him on the events of the day, even going so far as to tell him she was meeting Paul that evening. That information brought forth a black look and a frown.

"I don't like the idea," he said flatly.

Dee dared to be a little flirtatious. "What's the matter, Jason? A little jealous?"

He nodded. "You could say that. The guy's

a ladies' man. And deep down I think he's a creep."

"I can take care of myself," Dee told him.

"I hope so." He ran his hands through his dark hair. "Jennifer and Eileen are having an animated conversation in the kitchen. I tried to listen in, but I got shooed away."

"If only there were some way to make Nicholas talk to us without revealing to him that we think he's in danger!" Dee said forlornly.

"Maybe it's an overactive imagination on both our parts," Jason said hopefully. "He seems fairly unworried lately."

"I don't think it's just imagination." Dee shook her head as she caught sight of Steve's tall figure, dressed in bathing trunks, coming down to join them with a towel flung over his shoulders. "Well, here comes Steve."

Jason frowned again. "You're getting so popular I seldom have time to be with you anymore."

By that time Steve had reached them, and after a few strained words, Jason wandered down the beach.

Dee tried to enjoy her swim with the doctor, but her mind was on everything but Stephen Winthrop.

CHAPTER SEVEN

The night was very dark when Dee slipped out to meet Paul. Actually, it hadn't been necessary to slip away at all. Steve had gotten out of the way early, probably to leave Dee a clear path to her rendezvous with Paul. Jennifer had gone to bed in a huff, and Gilly followed her in a flurry of apologies. Jason was nowhere to be found, and it was an empty living room and terrace that Dee left to go down to the wharf.

Her footsteps seemed very loud on the white oyster-shell path, and she tried to walk more quietly, afraid to step off the path into the grass because of snakes. The sky was filled with low, brooding clouds. There had been some talk on the radio about a tropical storm trying to form in the ocean to the south, and the palm trees seemed to give off sinister rustlings as the cool breeze played around them.

Now and again Dee paused, for she felt sure she heard other footsteps besides her own. But when she stopped, they stopped, and she could be sure of nothing.

She had expected to see the outline of Paul's body against the sky as she neared the dock, but there was no sign of any other human being. Suddenly, Dee longed for the security of the house she had left behind and wondered why she had been so anxious to make this tryst in the dark.

"Paul?" she cried softly. "Paul, are you here?"

Now there was no mistake. She heard running footsteps in the woods behind her, and a faint groan coming from the wharf in front. Straining her eyes, she could make out a huddled form lying still on the worn planks. She wanted to run away herself, but her nurse's training restrained her, and she moved across the rough surface to the side of the prone figure. The heavy clouds parted for a moment, and she saw Paul's bright blond hair stained now with a darker substance that had to be blood.

Quickly falling to her knees, she felt for his pulse and thankfully found it strong and regular. He opened his eyes and stared up at her blankly, then lifted a hand to touch his forehead, wincing as he did so.

"What happened?" he asked huskily.

"I don't know. You tell me." Dee desperately wished for a light so she could see the extent of his injuries.

"I was just standing here waiting for you, Dee, when suddenly I felt as if a pile driver had hit me, and then there was nothing. When I came to, you were here leaning over me."

"Do you think you can stand?" Dee asked anxiously. "If you can't, I'll have to go for help. We have to get you back to the house."

He grinned painfully. "I'll try. Give me a hand."

Dee helped Paul to his feet, then grabbed for him as she felt him weaving slightly. "Are you all right?" she asked.

"Just a little dizzy, that's all. I think I can make it to the house now." Suddenly, he gave a little start and reached into the inside pocket of his coat. "The will! Someone stole it! It's gone!"

Dee gave a quick glance along the wharf.

"Are you sure you didn't drop it when you fell?"

"No way. You can see for yourself that it's not here. I guess whoever hit me on the head got what he wanted."

Gently Dee led Paul back along the path, encouraging him to lean on her. "How important was that will, Paul? Can you frame another?"

"It's the only signed copy, of course," Paul explained. "But I always keep copies. Losing it is only a delaying tactic. It just means I have to make another trip out here next week with a clean copy and have Nicholas sign it again."

"Paul, what's in that will that makes it so important?" Dee asked.

"You know I can't divulge that. I can only say there is no great change from the last one. There's no reason for anybody to feel threatened by it."

They had reached the steps, and Paul stopped a moment to get his breath, closing his eyes against his evident weakness.

"Thank you for telling me that much," Dee told him gratefully. "Now I'll help you to your room and I'll call Steve to have a look at you."

Steve was still dressed when Dee rapped

at his bedroom door. He grabbed his bag and came quickly. Paul was stretched out on his bed. He had taken off his shoes and suit coat, and Dee had put a towel on the pillow under his head.

Steve was quiet as he examined Paul. "There doesn't seem to be any evidence of concussion," the young doctor said at last, putting away the pencil-like light he had used to peer into Paul's eyes. "All we can do now is keep an ice pack on your head and look out for symptoms of drowsiness or disorientation."

Dee had brought in a basin and a clean cloth, and she was busy cleaning the wound. It seemed to look worse than it was because of the bleeding. Now she broke into the conversation, directing her words to Paul.

"Are you sure you didn't hear anything before you got the blow on your head?" she asked. "Anything at all?"

"Not a thing. I was just standing there in the darkness, looking out over the water, and the next thing I knew, you were bending over me," Paul said as Steve bandaged his head.

"And the only thing you found missing was the will?" Dee continued.

"Yes. My wallet is intact. And there's no problem in duplicating the will. It's just a matter of typing and having it signed and witnessed again."

"Then the old will would be valid, unless somebody came up with the new one," Dee said quietly.

Steve looked stern. "Then all the attacker has done is gain one more week until you return with the new will for Nick to sign."

"That's right," Paul answered. "It was hardly worth the headache—and I mean that literally!" He touched his newly bandaged head. "It's like I was telling Dee—I can't discuss the contents of the will, but I can tell you the changes are not great enough to motivate anything like this."

Steve said, "I suggest you try to get some rest, and I'll look in on you in the morning."

Paul gave Dee a wicked little grin. "I sure could use a good-looking nurse to sit with me all night."

"I think you'll survive without that," Dee told him lightly. "Nevertheless, I think you should lock your door and windows."

"I'll do that." Paul said suddenly sober and serious again.

Steve ushered her out of the room and led

her into his own. It was a masculine room,
and Dee caught the scent of pipe tobacco and
Steve's aftershave. As she sat down in one
of the room's two chairs, she smoothed the
folds of her pink cotton skirt, happy that for
once she wasn't in her starched uniform. As
Steve sat down across from her, she noticed
grim worry lines on his face.

"I'm really concerned," he began, his voice
rough. "Something's going on and I don't
like it."

"Do you have any suspicions of who might
have attacked Paul?" she asked him anxiously. "I heard footsteps running through
the woods when I heard him groan. It was
impossible for me to know who it was."

"It almost had to be somebody here on the
island. I think we can eliminate Jennifer
and Gilly since they're total outsiders."
Steve reached idly for his pipe, then began
to tamp tobacco into the bowl.

"But who does that leave? Just Eileen,
Bert, Jason, you, and me." Dee felt a little
sick.

"That's right. I know we'd both like to
think Bert did it—but that's because we
don't care for him personally, and that's not
a fair supposition. Of course, he would do
anything that his mother told him to do. But

again, we have to ask why." Steve paused.
"How has Jason really been getting along
with his grandfather?"

"Surely, you don't suspect him?" Dee
struggled with her outrage for a moment,
and then continued. "They are hitting it off
very well. I think I told you they've been
together every day."

"Has Jason ever told you why he's here?"
Steve asked curiously.

"I honestly think he wanted to check on
his grandfather's condition—and he mentioned wanting to borrow money from him."

Dee could see Steve stiffen. "That's totally
out of character!" he said positively.

Dee nodded. "I thought so, too. But why
would Jason want to attack Paul?"

"I don't think Paul is the key," Steve said
thoughtfully. "I think it's the will."

"After the way Nick carried on, I hate to
suggest it—but do you suppose Bert really
could be his son?" Dee looked perplexed.

"I find it hard to believe," Steve said
slowly. "But if that were true, it could explain the Powerses' interest in the will."

"And possibly Jason's, too, in all fairness,"
Dee admitted sickly. "He hates Bert and
Eileen."

Steve scowled. "I hate to say this, but I

think you should go back to the launch with me tomorrow. I don't like the things that are happening here."

"I'm safe enough," she said. "It isn't me somebody's after."

"But there's a chance they may be after Nicholas, and you could get in the way. Why bother to destroy the will today, when Nicholas will just sign it again next week?" Steve asked reluctantly.

"Do you seriously believe Mr. Wakeford's life may be in danger?" Dee had to struggle to keep the tremor out of her voice.

"I just don't know." Steve stood up and walked to the window. Parting the blinds, he looked out into the blackness. "I only know I don't want you in any danger."

She rose and walked over to join him. "And how about Nicholas? He's our patient, Steve—yours and mine. If he's in danger, we can't walk out on him. Either one of us."

Steve turned sharply, and she could see the concern in his eyes. "I brought you here, Dee, and I feel personally responsible because you've come to mean more to me than just another nurse. I can get a male nurse to take your place. I knew the situation here would be difficult, but I didn't plan on it being dangerous as well. I want you out of here."

She shook her head stubbornly. "I won't go," she said defiantly.

"Then I guess we'd better get to the bottom of this affair rapidly," he sighed as he walked to the door and opened it for her.

As she brushed past him, he reached out a hand to stop her. She was very near him, and his eyes were like two deep pools, pools in which she knew she would drown if she were not careful.

Gently both his hands came up to cup her face. "Lock your door and lock your windows," he said softly. "Be a little extra careful, Dee—for me."

His lips lowered toward hers, brushing them in a simple, quick kiss that was over almost before she knew it had happened. As Steve shut the door behind her, she turned, and a bit of movement at the end of the hall caught her eye. It was Jason. She could see he was furious at seeing her coming out of Steve's bedroom. She knew he had witnessed the kiss, as well.

She lifted her hand to stop him, to explain, but with fury in every line of his body, he swung around and strode away.

She would have to explain later. Wearily she went into her own room. She had a lot to think about that night.

Breakfast was strained and uncomfortable. Jason was still angry with Dee and didn't pretend otherwise. Paul was rather wan, despite his tan, and Steve got into an argument with Jennifer, who flatly refused to leave on the launch with him and Paul.

"I'm afraid you'll have to honor your host's request and go back to your magazine," Steve insisted hotly.

"Nicholas Wakeford is not my host in the strict sense of the word. I'm here on a business assignment, with his full agreement, and now he is refusing to keep his part of the bargain."

"He's an old man, and he's ill."

Jennifer had a subdued air of triumph about her. "At least I know the full story of his relationship with Eileen Powers and Bert," she taunted. "Do you? It's going to make one terrific story."

"I wouldn't advise you to tell any lies in your article," Steve threatened her. "There's a difference in supposition and fact."

Jennifer was condescending. "I'm an investigative reporter, and I know my job, Dr. Winthrop. I'm also onto some interesting facts about the old man's new will, and I won't leave here until I know more about it."

Steve finally raised his voice. "I want you off this island, today!"

Jennifer rose, gave him a scornful look, and took her coffee with her as she headed for her room.

Gilly got up to follow her automatically, but turned to the group before she left, flushed and apologetic.

"Jennifer can be very stubborn," she said unhappily, her eyes darting about as though she couldn't look anyone straight in the face. "I'm sorry if we're causing you any trouble. If it were up to me, I'd be glad to leave."

"It's all right, Gilly," Dee said quickly. "Nobody blames you."

"Thank you." The slender redhead followed her companion out of the room.

Eileen Powers entered the room as Gilly left, unobtrusively clearing away the breakfast dishes.

"What have you been telling Jennifer Lane?" Jason asked with an accusing tone in his voice.

"She asked, I answered," Eileen said stoically.

"You've never told me what your relationship is with my grandfather," Jason said angrily.

Eileen turned to him, her eyes furious, her face red except for two white parentheses enclosing her mouth. "And you never asked me decently!" she retorted. "You've always been too busy treating me like a servant, refusing to obey me, giving me nothing but trouble. You've never talked to me like a human being, and I have no desire to talk to you!"

She had shocked the group into silence. She piled the last dish on her tray and stalked out of the room, the swinging door to the kitchen giving mute testimony to her passing.

"Well!" Jason looked shocked. "There's a real person under that facade after all!"

"I wonder what she told Jennifer?" Dee asked quietly. "Maybe if you tried to talk to Eileen again—"

"No." Jason shook his head negatively. "I'm afraid the bridge between us cannot be mended. I hope you'll all excuse me, but I was up most of the night." He got to his feet, looking at Paul closely. "I'm sorry, but I'm curious. What is that rather large bandage doing on your head?"

"Somebody knocked me cold last night and stole your grandfather's new will," Paul answered directly.

Jason's swift gaze sought Dee. "So that's what you were doing in Winthrop's room last night."

"Yes, it was." Dee could see that part of the explanation was acceptable to Jason, but it didn't undo the kiss Jason had seen, and that still stood between them.

"I don't suppose you saw anybody around the wharf around nine-thirty or ten?" Dee asked.

"The wharf? No, that wasn't where I was." Jason's eyes narrowed. "So the plot thickens. I hope you feel better, Kennedy, and don't suffer any aftereffects."

"I'm sure I'll be fine," Paul answered pleasantly.

Jason's eyes touched Dee's again. "I'll see you later," he promised, and Dee knew there were unspoken meanings in the innocuous words.

Jason's departure left only the three of them in the dining room—Steve, Paul, and Dee. There was a worried frown on Steve's face.

"I still feel reluctant to leave you here alone," he confessed. "Too much is happening. I'm sure you are also aware that there's a tropical storm brewing in the Gulf. If it comes this way, it might be wise to evacuate Nicholas. I'd like you to stay in daily communication with me, if you will."

"Perhaps it might be better for you to call me," Dee returned. "I'm not that sure of your schedule."

"I'll be coming back along with Steve next weekend," Paul offered. "I have to bring the new will." He rose, looking about him curiously. "What's the latest on the progress of the storm?"

"I haven't heard the morning news," Steve admitted. "There's a shortwave in my room. I'll turn it on when I go to pack."

"I'd better get my things together as well," Paul said. "I'll see you again before we leave, Dee."

"Of course." She inclined her head graciously as the two men went their respective ways.

Having the men on the island had been a pleasant break in the monotony for Dee, before the attack on Paul made her realize there was definitely someone on the island who wasn't at all what he or she seemed to be on the surface.

Dee stepped out on the terrace sometime later, noting that the sky was overcast with low, scudding clouds. The temperature seemed to have dropped several degrees. The jeep was parked in the drive, obviously left there by Bert to pick up the luggage that had to go back to the mainland on the launch.

She realized Jason must be sleeping after his surveillance of the night before. He would have been somewhere on the grounds at the time Paul was attacked. Bert could have been anywhere, for he kept a very low profile when the other men were around. Steve had ostensibly been in his room. Eileen was in her apartment at the back of the house.

Dee discounted Jennifer and Gilly, but they had no better alibi than the others. And somebody had taken the will from Paul. Dee remembered, with a shudder, the footsteps she had heard running away from the wharf. She had been very near Paul's attacker. If she had been one minute earlier, she might have found the perpetrator in the act.

"Dee?" The small voice behind her surprised her, made her turn swiftly.

It was Gilly Jones, and she seemed distressed, folding and unfolding her hands nervously.

"Hello, Gilly." Dee tried to smile pleasantly. "Would you like me to call Bert to get your things?"

"That's just it. Jennifer's gone. She just took off through the woods. She says she isn't going back until she's good and ready. I don't like to cause trouble. I wish she would just go!"

Gilly looked as though she might break into tears at any moment. Dee felt a sudden pity for her, overshadowed by Jennifer as she was.

"Surely, she will come back in time to take the launch after all," Dee said, trying to convince herself at the same time.

"No." Gilly was adamant. "You don't know how stubborn she can be. When she says something, she means it."

"I'll see what I can do."

Dee left her standing on the terrace and went to Steve's room to acquaint him with the latest development.

Steve was just closing his overnight case. Dee's news made him frown angrily. "This island isn't very large," he said, "but if someone really wants to hide, it could take forever to find them." He picked up his suitcase and took his medical bag with the other hand. "We'll see what Bert has to say." He

stood back for Dee to lead the way, then
followed her to the front veranda.

Bert was standing by the jeep, his face a
thundercloud. Paul was already inside. Gilly
was standing on the steps, weeping and
wringing her hands.

"Jennifer says she's found out something
about the will," Gilly said helplessly. "She
won't leave until she finds out more about
it. She's always like that. Like a bulldog,
always hanging on. I can't help it. I just
can't help it."

"We've waited long enough, Dr. Winthrop," Bert said shortly. "The Gulf's pretty
choppy today. I'd like to get to the mainland
and come back early."

Frustrated, Steve slammed his bags into
the back of the jeep. "It's all right, Gilly,"
he said tiredly. "Nobody's blaming you." He
came around the jeep and paused beside Dee.
"Be careful," he warned her. "I'll be back
early in the week, especially if there's a need
to evacuate Nick. Call me every day. Or I'll
try to call you. I want to know what's happening here."

"I will." Dee's hands felt ice cold.

She almost wanted to throw her arms
around Steve and beg him not to go, but she

knew she couldn't. Instead, she watched as the jeep drove down the oyster-shell path. Gilly had already disappeared into the interior of the house. Dee felt very much alone again.

The launch had dwindled to a speck when Dee became aware that someone else was on the terrace with her. She turned slowly to see Jason glowering at her.

"I couldn't sleep much," he said crossly. "Have they gone?"

Dee gestured toward the wide expanse of water. "They're out of sight now."

"Did the magazine people go with them?"

Dee shook her head negatively. "Jennifer managed to stay out of the way until they left."

Jason sat down, looking thoroughly miserable. "I have to know what's going on between you and Steve Winthrop," he burst out suddenly. "I saw him kissing you last night, and I haven't been able to think about anything else since."

"It was just a friendly kiss," Dee protested. "I was upset, and he was trying to comfort me."

Jason looked down like a shamed little boy. "I'm in love with you, Dee," he managed to say at last. "It isn't that I'm just physi-

cally attracted to you. It's a lot more. You're
sweet, and you're gentle, and you have a lot
of kindness and patience in you. All that
comes out when you're with Nick. I know
we don't know each other very well—but I
need to know there's time to rectify that. I
want to marry you—and I've never said that
to any other girl."

Dee looked at him in amazement. "But
you don't really know me! We haven't been
together long enough to think about such a
lasting step."

He nodded. "I know that. I just admitted
as much. All I'm asking you to do is tell me
there's a chance—that you aren't committed to anyone else."

Dee knew Jason deserved a truthful answer. "I'm not committed to Steve, if that's
what you mean," she said. "I'm fond of him,
but I think I'm fonder of you. Does that answer your question?"

His eyes lighted up as he leapt to his feet
and hugged her, sweeping her off her feet
in his exuberance.

"I love you, Dee," he chortled. "I do, and
you're going to love me, too!"

"We'll see." She grinned. "Now put me
down, Jason, you big oaf!"

They were still laughing when the sound

of Jennifer's voice interrupted them.

"This is a touching little scene," she said snidely.

They both stopped to look at her. She had obviously just walked onto the terrace. Her straw-colored hair clung to her forehead in damp tendrils, and there were grass stains on her neat white canvas shoes. Dee wondered where she had been hiding and then decided she didn't care.

"You missed the launch," she said flatly.

"I intended to," Jennifer said. "I still have work to do. I've heard some very interesting things from Mrs. Powers. Now I need to talk to Bert. Maybe then I'll take my leave of your sticky little island."

"We can't wait," Jason said.

Jennifer turned without a word and flounced into the house through the glass doors.

CHAPTER EIGHT

Dee rose early the next morning, aware of an eerie stillness in the air. The clouds hung low, hovering darkly, churning and angry. Sleep still clung to her, and she found it difficult to concentrate on anything. She moved on leaden feet through the silent house, pausing before Nicholas's door to take a deep breath and draw the cloak of professionalism about her.

When she opened the door, she was surprised to find Nick sitting up in bed, pouring some water from the carafe near the bell on his bedside table. In his hand he held one of the little paper cups Dee used to give him his medication.

"What are you doing?" she asked sharply.

"Taking this confounded medication!" he

barked in return. "I thought I might be spared seeing you this morning, since you finally decided to be sensible and leave the pills for me."

"I didn't leave these for you," she said, examing the two pills in the bottom of the fluted cup.

"Humph!" Nick snorted. "I should have known better, Miss Know-It-All. I think you enjoy waking me up every morning."

Dee was still staring at the pills. They were similar in shape and size to the ones she gave him every morning, but something told her these were different. Very different.

"What woke you up? You're never awake at this time of morning." Dee busied herself shaking two more pills out, into another fluted cup, from the bottle she had in her pocket. Wordlessly she offered them to him and he swallowed them, his wrinkled neck moving like the wattles of a turkey.

"I don't know what woke me," he said irritably. "A noise, I think. Then, when I saw the medication there waiting for me, I just reached for it. If you didn't leave it, then who did?"

"I don't know." Dee leaned over him, bringing her eyes on a level with his. "Don't take any medicine you don't get from my hands, Mr. Wakeford. Please."

His brow wrinkled as he eyed her keenly. "You trying to tell me something, Crawford?"

"Just do as I say. Promise me."

"All right. Just go away and let me sleep."

"No sooner said than done," Dee answered and left him alone in the big bed.

She clutched the pills she had taken from him in one hand as she raced back to her room. She was convinced somebody had tried to poison the old man. The pills looked innocent enough, but they were totally unfamiliar to Dee. She was acquainted with most ordinary medications. These had the stamp of a laboratory she had never heard of before.

She dropped them into a little plastic envelope and tucked it into her pocket. She had to call Steve, and soon. She dared not confide in anybody on the island, for one of them had placed the pills on Nick's bedside table. The question was who?

The house was still deserted as she made her way to the wireless phone to call Steve. It was too early to reach him at the office, so she got him at home.

The sound of his voice was welcome. Dee explained what had happened with an economy of words, and Steve was just as upset as she had thought he would be.

"What do the pills look like?" he asked tersely. "Describe them to me."

Dee reached into her pocket and pulled out the envelope, describing the pills as well as she could, even down to the raised letters on them. The connection between them was excellent, for Dee could easily hear his quick intake of breath.

"I hope they're not what I think they are," he said, seeming worried. "They could be a very strong heart stimulant—strong enough to send Nick into a massive heart attack."

"Then thank heaven I got to him in time," Dee said with a catch in her voice.

"I'll have to see them and test them to be sure," Steve continued. "Take care of them until I get there. The early-morning news says the hurricane is headed directly for you. I don't want to wait. If you'll send Bert over with the launch, I'll come back with him and we'll move Nicholas off the island."

"Why don't I pack him up and bring him myself? There's no sense in Bert making two trips," Dee said.

"I think I ought to be with him. The trip could be hard on him, for the seas are choppy. He may need some attention on the way."

"All right." Dee knew Steve was right. "I'll find Bert and get him on his way immediately."

Suddenly, before the connection was broken, Jason was in the room, without Dee realizing he had come in. Dee gave a little start, wondering if it was her nerves or shadows that made his face look faintly menacing.

"I couldn't help but overhear you," Jason said shortly. "You won't find Bert this morning. He didn't come back yesterday, and the launch is missing."

"What's that?" Steve demanded sharply over the phone. "What did he say?"

"He said Bert never came back yesterday. Do you think he decided to stay over on the mainland?" Dee asked nervously.

"No, I don't," Steve replied. "I passed the marina late last night and the launch was gone. It's not at Galena."

"I hope he didn't run into trouble." Dee hated to think what could have happened to Bert on the angry sea. "I wonder why Mrs. Powers hasn't said anything. You'd think she'd be frantic."

"Bert has his own place," Steve answered. "An apartment over the garage and storage shed not far from the house. She may not know he hasn't returned."

"Tell Winthrop I'll take my boat and come for him," Jason ordered. "Have him notify the Coast Guard about Bert and have him meet me at the Galena marina in a couple of hours. We'll get Nicholas off the island this afternoon in my boat. We'd better hurry, for the wind is starting to rise out there."

Dee repeated his words to Steve as Jason left the room.

"I suppose that's best," Steve said hesitantly. "But it's going to pose something of a problem. We'll have to have Jason, of course, to run the boat, and there's still you, me, Nick, the *Achievement Magazine* people, and Eileen Powers to evacuate as well. That's too many people for Jason's boat. You'd better start praying that Bert returns safely. And you'd better tell Eileen he's missing. That's one chore I don't envy you."

Dee had to steel herself to hang up the phone and break the tenuous line of communication between them.

Her hands felt clammy and she wiped them on the sides of her uniform. Slowly, on leaden feet, she made her way to the kitchen, looking for Eileen. The housekeeper was there, busily preparing the morning coffee and taking eggs out of the refrigerator.

Dee swallowed and tried to speak gently. "Mrs. Powers, Bert hasn't returned with the launch."

Eileen reached into the refrigerator for the butter and set it out on the counter. "Don't you think I know that?" she asked sharply.

"Aren't you worried about him?" Dee was surprised at the housekeeper's reaction.

"Why? Bert can take care of himself." Eileen took a big frying pan from the cabinet and placed it calmly on the stove.

"There's a hurricane coming," Dee said. "We need the launch to take Mr. Wakeford to the mainland."

"Bert'll be back in plenty of time to shore up the house," Eileen said positively. "We've ridden out hurricanes before. There's no need to evacuate. Bert knows that. You'd be risking Mr. Wakeford's life for nothing."

"I can't understand your calmness," Dee said. "I should think you'd be screaming for the Coast Guard!"

Eileen glared at Dee, holding the frying

pan almost like a weapon. "Don't you go setting anybody on my boy's trail," she said angrily. "Bert knows what he's doing on the water, and if he isn't back, there's a good reason. He'll be here. You'll see."

In view of Eileen's anger, Dee decided it was better not to tell her that Steve had doubtless already notified the Coast Guard.

Jason came in for coffee, his cheeks reddened by the wind. "It's really dark out there," he announced. "I'll be taking off in just a minute. Have you seen Jennifer or Gilly?"

"They're in the living room, putting up a clamor for their breakfast," Eileen said sourly.

Dee poured herself a cup of coffee as well and followed Jason to the living room where the two women from *Achievement Magazine* were standing, looking out of the glass doors over the terrace to the twisting palm trees and live-oak limbs. Both of them were dressed in jeans and T-shirts. They turned in unison as Jason came in with Dee.

"It's blowing up out there," Jason said. "I'm taking my boat over to Galena to pick up Dr. Winthrop. We plan to evacuate Nicholas as soon as we return. Now you're

both welcome to make the trip with me, because there'll be no room on the second trip.
I'm warning you now."

Jennifer's eyes flashed. "You aren't getting rid of me that easily, and you can't scare
me. These hurricanes never hit where
they're forecast to strike. I told you I have
to talk to Bert Powers before I go."

Gilly touched the writer's arm. "Please,
Jennifer," she said softly. "I think we ought
to go with him."

Jason suddenly seemed to lose patience.
"If you want to go, Gilly, why can't you stand
up to Jennifer just once and do what you
think is best? But make up your mind, because I'm leaving now!"

Gilly seemed to shrink. "All right. I'll stay.
I'm sorry."

Jason shook his head in disgust. "Well,
I've no time to argue with you. Dee, be sure
Nicholas is ready. We won't have much time
when I return."

He grabbed her in a hard embrace and
gave her a rough kiss before he marched to
the door and exited into the morning gray-
ness. It was strange to see no sight of the
sun. Usually, by this time, it was high in
the sky.

"I hope you won't be sorry you didn't take Jason up on his offer," Dee said curtly before she turned and marched away as well, determined to pack Nicholas's things and get him dressed in warm clothing for the necessary evacuation.

The time seemed to fly. Dee packed a few of her own things, too, changing from her uniform to sturdy tan slacks and a heavy sweat shirt. The envelope with the pills she put deep in her trouser pocket for Steve to see.

Searching through the closets near the back door, she found some good heavy rain gear and lugged it to the front door in readiness. She was thankful for the wheelchair that made it so much easier for her to manipulate Nicholas. As she worked, she kept listening for the sound of the boat returning, but the noise of the waves seemed to block everything else out.

It was almost like an anticlimax when Jason and Steve arrived at long last.

"The water's really choppy," Jason announced as they entered. "I figure we have three, four hours at the most before it will be impassable."

Steve busied himself getting Nicholas into

the wheelchair, nodding approvingly at the arrangements Dee had made. Nicholas was his usual argumentative self.

"All of this is utter nonsense," he snapped. "This house and this island have withstood worse blows than the one that's stirring up out there now."

Jason shook his head. "We can't go off and leave those other three women to fend for themselves," he said raggedly. "It will make for heavy going, but we have to take them with us."

"I can assure you that Mrs. Powers will not go," Nicholas said staunchly. "I am sure, as she is, that Bert will get back here in time to board up the house. But even if he doesn't, Mrs. Powers is capable of doing it herself. We have storm shutters that fit very easily over the windows. She'll be safe. It's us, bobbing about in a boat at sea, that you ought to be worried about."

The three of them escorted Nicholas from the room in his wheelchair, Steve pushing him, and Jason and Dee carrying his bags.

When they passed the living room, Eileen came to stand before them, looking forbidding. "You're making a mistake, Mr. Wakeford," she told him harshly. "Bert will be

back to see to us as he always has. These
people will only lead you to your death!"

Nick chortled. "I told them you wouldn't
go along with them," he said triumphantly.

Dee's eyes traveled around the room and
stopped on Gilly, huddled miserably in an
armchair. At her feet was a small overnight
bag.

"I've changed my mind," Gilly said in a
small voice. "I'm going back with you."

"You aren't going anywhere!" Jennifer
said. She had just come in from the terrace.
Now she turned to Jason. "Your boat's gone.
I just saw it drifting out to sea."

"What?" In a burst of outrage, Jason ran
past her, shoving her aside rudely, heading
for the wharf.

Dee looked at Jennifer in disbelief. "What
have you done?" she gasped. "Did you untie
that boat and let it drift?"

Jennifer smiled, a slow, sultry smile. "I
probably would have, if I had thought of
it—but, no, it was already out beyond the
breakers when I went to the wharf. Looks
like we're all in this together, mates." Insolently she turned to Gilly. "Get me some
coffee, will you? It's a little cool out there."

Gilly got to her feet, her face flushed. She

opened her mouth to speak several times before the words came out, loud and clear. "If you want coffee, get it yourself. And if you cast off the line of that boat, I hope you get what's coming to you!"

Jennifer's eyes widened with surprise. "Ah, the mouse that roared!" she chuckled. "You'd better watch that insolence, my girl."

"I don't have to watch anything anymore. I quit doing assignments with you!" Her whole body took on an air of defiance. "I've had enough out of you, Jennifer Lane!"

"Atta girl," Steve murmured appreciatively, but so softly that only Dee heard him.

The wind blew into the room, making the curtains dance, as Jason came back from the wharf. He shook his head in disgust. "The boat's gone," he said flatly. "It was too far out for me to rescue." He gave Steve a piercing glance. "We're stuck here now. All of us. Even if Bert comes back, it will be too late."

"All a bunch of nonsense, anyway," Nicholas grumbled. "Nonsense, I say!"

Steve relinquished the wheelchair to Dee. "Take Mr. Wakeford back to his room and make him comfortable," he told her. "Jason and I had better see to securing the house."

Jason was glaring at Jennifer with a look

that bordered on hatred. "If I ever find out
you're responsible for this, you're going to
pay for it," he said coldly.

"You really scare me," Jennifer said, her
voice heavy with sarcasm. "I really didn't
do anything to your old boat, you know."

Dee rolled Nicholas back to his room, nervous and shaken. Fate did not want them
to leave this island until all the scenes had
been played, until this drama came to an
inevitable end. She helped the old man un-
dress and get back into his bed, realizing he
was exhausted from the unaccustomed excitement.

Outside, she could hear the banging of
hammers and the voices of the two men as
they called back and forth to each other.

"What are they doing?" she asked
Nicholas curiously.

"There are storm shutters for every window and outside door to the house," Nick
replied. "We keep them stored in the space
under Bert's place. He has his own apartment, you know."

"Yes, I know," she said softly as she covered the old man. Then she closed the door
gently behind her and went out to see if she
could be of any assistance to the two men.

They were bringing the shutters from a sturdy concrete block building set back in the jungle-like foliage. Dee had seen it often, but had surmised it was only used to garage the jeep. Now she noticed the second story that Bert used for his living quarters.

Dee joined the men, carrying the shutters and helping to hold them in place while Steve and Jason bolted them down. Nervously she asked Jason what he thought would happen.

"Some of these blows can be quite nasty," he told her. "The water comes up so high you'd think it would sweep over the island, but so far it never has. The house is sturdy and well built. It's weathered these storms before."

Shivering, Dee looked down at the angry Gulf. The waters were slate-gray, echoing the darkness of the clouds above. Already the waves were breaking angrily upon the wharf, threatening to sweep it away with their angry might.

"Did you call the Coast Guard about Bert?" Dee asked Steve anxiously. He was perched on top of a stepladder, wielding a screwdriver. "I hope he's not out on the water in that launch."

Steve's lips tightened as he descended. "I called them," he said simply. "They said they'd be on the lookout for him. There's really nothing else we can do but batten down and ride this thing out."

"It's a shame you're trapped here as well," Dee said almost apologetically. "If it weren't for Mr. Wakeford—"

"Hush. I'd rather be here, if there's a question of your being isolated. We'll wait the storm out in fine condition. You'll see." He lifted the ladder and moved down to the next window. Dee followed him like his shadow.

Eileen appeared on the terrace, her hands jammed into her apron pockets. "There's work to do inside, Miss Crawford," she said harshly. "I really don't think the men need your help as much as I do."

Sighing, Dee went to meet Eileen. "What can I do to help?" she asked, somehow pleased that, for once, Eileen Powers had asked for assistance.

"We need to run a supply of drinking water before the wells become contaminated," the older woman told her. "At least two bathtubs should be filled. Then there is hot coffee and tea to be prepared and stored in thermos containers. Soup, too, in case we have no electricity. There are a couple of roasts we can cook, and a turkey. It may be a while before things get back to normal."

Dee followed Mrs. Powers inside and found, to her surprise, that Gilly was already working diligently in the kitchen. Mrs. Powers was right. There was a lot to do. Fortunately, most of it was done by the time Nicholas rang his little silver bell for attention.

Dee had just set up his table for a late-afternoon meal when a bolt of lightning slashed through the air, leaving a distinct smell of ozone. Shortly afterward, there was a crash of thunder and the house shook. Then the heavens opened and a deluge of rain began to fall.

Dee could hear it, though she couldn't see it through the closed shutters. Nicholas indicated the window proudly. "Good boy, that Bert. I knew he'd get us shipshape in no time."

Dee couldn't tell him that Bert was still missing, lost on that lonely sea. It was better that the old man not worry. Dee sat with him until he finished eating, feeling the tension rising within her as the storm increased in fury. She tucked him back in bed with a book, making sure there was a fat candle and a box of matches on his bedside table.

Downstairs, Eileen had prepared a hot meal, and the five of them sat around the table trying to eat heartily. Dee kept glancing at Eileen, wondering just what was going on in her mind. Surely, she was worried about Bert, but if she was, Dee saw no evidence of it.

Even the hurricane wasn't enough to make the woman relax her formality. She stood in the kitchen door like a graven statue, watching the rest of them eat.

Outside, the winds were rising. Every so often, something struck the house with a resounding blow. Dee supposed they were tree limbs, wrenched from their trunks by the twisting, tearing wind. The little group around the table was morose and silent, finding it hard to make conversation.

Finally, Jennifer rose jerkily to her feet. "I think I'll take a hot shower while I'm sure we have water. Want to come along, Gilly?"

Gilly shook her head. "I've never been in a hurricane before. There's space between the shutters to peep out at the storm through the glass doors. I'd like to see what I can."

"Just don't open the doors," Jason warned her sharply. "I'll check around the house and make sure no water is leaking through the windows. The wind is really slashing the water against the house."

"How was Nicholas when you left him?" Steve asked Dee.

"Resting. Perhaps he should have a sedative to help him sleep through the night," Dee answered.

"I'll take care of it." Steve reached for his black bag. "Are you coming?"

"No. I thought I'd help Mrs. Powers clear the table." Dee rose to her feet.

Eileen Powers looked at her with no change of expression. "How many times do I have to tell you that the kitchen is my responsibility?" she asked.

Dee considered herself properly chastised. "Then I think I'll go to my room for a change of clothing," she announced. "Maybe I'll take a shower, too. It's going to be a long night."

Dee's room looked strange with the windows blocked and no welcoming view outside. The rush of wind made thinking difficult, and it seemed she could hear the roar of the breakers from the beach. Dee wished with all her heart that they were all safe on the mainland. They could have been, had it not been for Jason's missing boat. She wondered just what had really happened to that boat. Had it slipped its moorings, or had Jennifer set it free? Either way, they were marooned here, and they had to make the best of it.

The lightning was flashing intermittently at the windows, and the thunder was becoming almost constant. If Bert were out there, he was dead. Dee was sure of it, and she failed to see how Eileen could be so complacent about it.

Dee stepped quickly into her shower, grateful for the hot water that beat down on her tired muscles. They had a long way to go before this would be over. She dried herself quickly and slipped into blue jeans and a long-sleeved plush shirt. She had just brushed back her hair and fastened it with two barrettes when a sharp bolt of lightning and a crashing crescendo of thunder made the lights flicker and then go out.

The darkness was complete. Dee groped for the candle she knew she had placed by the bed and scratched a match with shaking fingers. She almost burned herself lighting the wick when a loud, keening scream came to her ears.

She grabbed the candle, protecting the flame with her other hand as the loud scream came again. Racing for the door, she came into the hall to see candle flames converging like fireflies, massing before Jennifer's door. Each of the burning candles threw eerie shadows on the faces of the people who carried them.

Dee heard Gilly moaning as she forced her way into the forefront of the group. By the light of the massed candles, aided by the flash of the lightning from a window, Dee could see Jennifer sprawled in an unseemly heap on her bed, her straw-colored hair fanned out beneath her, her green satin robe wrapped tightly about her body.

At first Dee thought Jennifer was wearing a red scarf at her throat. Then the lightning flashed again and she realized what she was seeing was the red of blood.

There was a knife buried in Jennifer's throat. Dee hurried to her side, conscious of someone else close beside her. It was Steve. He reached for a pulse, obviously found none. There was no hope for Jennifer. She was dead, her life poured out from the wound in her throat.

Dee felt numb, nerveless, as though she was standing above all this, displaced from it, as though these people were strangers and these events taking place on a motion-picture screen. She wondered about the brightness of the lightning and then realized one shutter was hanging loosely on the outside of its window, letting the lightning in at will. As it flashed, Dee saw wet footprints leading from the bed across the rug to the low sill.

Wordlessly Dee took her candle and gestured toward the unshuttered window. The bushes outside were weaving in a grotesque dance. Then, in a brilliant flash of lightning, they all saw the huddled outline of a man, stooped against the driving force of the storm, his hair wet and plastered against his face.

"Bert!" Eileen cried, giving a name to the apparition. "Bert's out there!"

Dee was aware of running footsteps, of events happening in a blur of time.

"Get me more light," Steve demanded, and Dee turned to do so, gathering candles from those who had gathered in the doorway.

Even as she lined them up and ordered

someone to bring the candlesticks from the dining room, she realized Jason was not among those who had responded to Jennifer's death scream.

CHAPTER NINE

Dee kept herding everyone out of the room, ordering them to look for more candles to light the rest of the house. "We can't leave Jennifer here like this," Dee said weakly, motioning to the prone body of the reporter.

"I'm afraid we must," Steve said, tight-lipped. "Heaven knows when the authorities will be able to get here. We'll disturb as little as possible, and just throw a cover over her. It would be a mistake to clean her up or move the body."

"It seems so callous to leave her just lying there." Dee shuddered. "It seems so cruel somehow."

"There is nothing dignified about murder," Steve said grimly. "Have you given

146

any thought as to who did it?"

As he spoke, he pulled a dull red blanket out of the closet. Without speaking, Dee approved of his choice. At least the bloodstains wouldn't show if they seeped through. A noise at the window made her look up sharply, to see the shutter being nailed back across the opening by some unseen person outside.

"It had to be Bert," she said dully. "You saw the wet footprints, and you saw him, too, didn't you? Standing out there in the wind and the rain?"

Steve cleared his throat. "I thought I did, yes," he admitted.

"None of us have an alibi," Dee said sickly. "We were all alone when it happened, I guess, and in the dark, it was hard to see just who responded immediately to the screams."

"But why Jennifer?" Steve asked. "What on earth could she have to do with anything?"

Dee clenched her teeth to keep them from chattering. "With all her talk about the will—what she knew about it—well, maybe she signed her own death warrant."

Jennifer's body had been covered, and a candle placed beside the bed, when the door opened and Jason entered, wet and dripping, blood oozing from a cut on his cheek.

"There was no sign of Bert when I got out there," he said tensely. "I don't see how he could remain upright out there, much less survive! I managed to get the shutter back on the window because I had to, but it took every ounce of strength I had to do it!"

"Then—you were here—you saw him, too?" Dee asked stupidly.

"Of course, I was here! Where did you think I was?" He looked at her with sudden suspicion. "Oh—you think it might have been me who thrust the knife into Jennifer's throat?"

Dee colored even as she denied it. "No, I don't!" she protested, but she could see Jason had been wounded by her suspicions.

"The two of you had better go in to see Grandfather," Jason told them coldly. "He's ringing his silver bell like a madman."

Dee tried to pull herself together. For once, she had almost forgotten her patient. It was only natural that he would be upset, in the dark, with the piercing screams and the hurrying footsteps in the hall.

Steve had gathered up all the candles but one and was taking them out as he spoke to Jason. "You'd better get into some dry clothes. We don't want a case of pneumonia on our hands."

Jason wouldn't even look at Dee as he took the candles from Steve and disappeared into the dark.

Jason was right. The sound of the little silver bell resounded through the hall. Dee and Steve hurried as fast as they could, by the light of their lone candle, to find Nicholas angry and fuming.

He had managed to light his own candle, so it was easy to see the craggy lines of his face and the piercing eyes under the shaggy eyebrows.

"What's going on out there?" he roared.

"I'm afraid the storm frightened one of our guests," Dee said soothingly.

"Don't treat me like a child!" Nicholas raged. "That unpleasant young woman got herself killed, didn't she? I may be old, but I'm not deaf!"

"All right," Dee said finally. "You're right. She did."

"Now will you two kindly explain what's going on in this house? My blood pressure rises a lot faster when I'm frustrated. This is my island, and I'm a lot stronger than you give me credit for. Now out with it!"

Steve sighed. "All right, Mr. Wakeford." He pulled up a chair near the bed and indicated that Dee was to do the same. "We've been trying to protect you, but I'm afraid it's a little late for that. Maybe it's time to be honest."

"Past time," Nicholas muttered.

Quickly, condensing the facts as much as possible, Steve ran down all the occurrences that had led him to believe Nicholas's life was seriously in danger.

"I really feel it's time you revealed what changes you made in your will that might have stirred up such violence, and time to tell us what your real relationship is to the Powerses. It might help us get a handle on this thing. You'll have to open up to the police anyway."

Nicholas nodded slowly. "Nothing changes for Eileen and Bert. I've always intended to leave this house and this island to Eileen and her son for the length of their lifetimes, along with an income to maintain it. That's never been a secret. Even Jason agrees with it." He sighed. "Blood's thicker than water, you know. I've feuded with Jason long enough. I had cut him out of my will with a small bequest, hoping I might bring him to his senses. I had willed the rest to various charities. All I changed was to leave everything to Jason instead—everything save what I had set aside for the Powers family anyway. I can't see why that sort of change would have affected anybody, other than the charities involved. There's certainly no motive for murder there."

Dee shook her head helplessly. "You're right. But there has to be an answer somewhere. Would you mind telling us what your relationship is with Mrs. Powers and Bert? Perhaps the answer lies there."

Nicholas nodded slowly. The flickering candlelight played on his features, making him seem older and tireder than he was. "All right," he said at last, his voice rumbling in his chest. As he talked, they sometimes had to strain to hear him above the muted roar of the storm outside.

"It pains me to talk of the past," he admitted. "At the time I married Gwyndolyn, I had a close friend. His name was Calvin Powers, and he worked for me. Though considerably younger than me, he was a dear friend—a close friend. During the first year of my marriage, Alex—Jason's father—was born.

"By the time Alex was six, Calvin no

longer worked for me but had branched out on his own. He met a woman—Eileen Stone, she was then—and they both wanted my family to be at their wedding. That was the story behind the letter Jennifer Lane found in my files."

Nicholas paused as though it pained him to go on. The house shook as a flying object struck its stone side with bruising force.

"We met intermittently over the next few years," Nick continued. "It was a great sorrow to both Eileen and Calvin that their marriage had not borne fruit. They were still childless." He reached for a glass of water, and Dee saw that his hand was shaking slightly, a mute testimony to the strain the old man was undergoing by reliving the past.

"The end came during a storm at sea," Nicholas said, his eyes dead orbs in his face. "We were all together on my boat, spending a long weekend just cruising about the islands. Weather forecasting was not the fine art it is today, and the storm that hit us was totally unexpected. In no time at all, the boat was crippled, and we knew she was going down.

"Calvin managed to lower the small rowboat we kept aboard for fishing in shallow waters. Gwyn put Alex in my arms and admonished me to hold him tight. We all managed the transfer into the rowboat fine — all but Gwyn. Her foot caught in a loop of rope just as a gigantic wave hit us, and she was swept overboard just as the big boat began to capsize.

"I had all I could do to hang on to the terrified child. Even so, I tried to free myself from him when I heard Gwyn's terrified screams, but the boy held me with the strength of ten demons. We all saw Gwyn there in the water, struggling."

A hand went up to cover the old eyes as the man's voice thickened, and Dee realized he was overcome by his memories. Without conscious thought, she gently touched him on one bent shoulder. When he looked up again, the ancient eyes were filled with tears.

"Those were shark-infested waters. All of us saw the dorsal fin as it cut through the water, heading straight for Gwyn. I tried again to push Alex away from me, to hand him to Calvin, but he was plastered to my body with a strength born of desperation.

"Calvin was the one who went over the

side, diving for her. For a few moments we thought he might make it—might actually manage her rescue. But then we heard his screams, saw him flailing about in the water, saw the red of his blood as it welled up around him. Then Gwyn disappeared under the waves. The look in her eyes as she went under!" Nicholas gave a deep, shuddering sigh. "The look in her eyes!"

"Go on," Dee said softly, trying to lead him past the terrible memory. "What happened then?"

"I finally managed to give the child to Eileen. I dove into the debris-filled water and managed to get my hands on Calvin. He was only half a man. Both legs were gone, sliced off by the shark's teeth. There was no sign of Gwyn. She was gone."

"I'm so sorry," Dee whispered.

"Now you know why I can't bear to talk about her," Nicholas continued gruffly. "The woman I loved lies in a watery grave, unmarked, after suffering a horrible death. But Calvin tried to save her. Gave up his legs trying to save her. Remember that."

"What happened to him?" Steve asked at last.

"We were in that devilish rowboat for

hours, at the mercy of the wind and the sea. Calvin was unconscious from shock and loss of blood. Eileen used my belt as a tourniquet to control the bleeding. I was in such a state of shock that it seemed I could feel nothing, do nothing. Once we were rescued, I saw to it that Calvin had the finest of medical attention. At least he survived."

Dee shivered. The story had been a horrible one, told as it was to the accompaniment of howling winds and lashing rain, punctuated by bolts of lightning and a background of rumbling thunder. Nicholas seemed white and exhausted, as though the effort of remembering had been too much for him.

"Thank you for telling us," Steve said at last. "Are you strong enough to tell us the rest of it? How Eileen and Bert came to live here on the island?"

The candle flickered dimly in a gust of wind. "I took good care of them," Nicholas explained. "It was the least I could do. Calvin had a fierce pride, and he was determined to work as much as he could in his condition. He never knew how much I did for the family, for Eileen and I entered into a conspiracy of silence. Alex was grown before Calvin

finally died, quietly, one night in his sleep."
Nicholas paused a moment, his eyes looking
back into the past. "Eileen was pregnant at
last—something they had both wanted, and
now it was too late for Calvin. It was ironic.
He never saw the child he craved so much.
I brought Eileen here, to the island. Her
child, Bert, was born here. Because of Calvin Powers, they will have a home here as
long as they live, and an income sufficient
to their needs. I have seen to that."

"And Jason doesn't know this story?"
Steve said.

"I told you I don't like to talk about it. It's
too painful." The old man's voice was getting weaker and he looked exhausted. "If
you could have seen Gwyn's face as she went
under. If you could have seen her face!"

"Well, it's over now," Dee said quickly.
"Steve will give you something to help you
sleep. Does the sound of the storm bother
you?"

"I hate storms," Nick confessed. "They
bring back the old memories all too vividly."

Dee and Steve worked in companionable
silence as they prepared Nicholas for sleep.
Now and again one of them spoke in a soothing voice to their patient, but they didn't

speak to each other until they were out in
the hall, their faces lit only by the light of
the flickering candle between them.

"It's Bert," Dee whispered sharply. "It has
to be Bert who's responsible for all of this."

"But why? And how is he surviving out
there in that storm?" Steve asked.

"I'm sure he's taken shelter in his own
place," Dee answered. "He must think
Nicholas is taking the island away from him
by changing the will. That means he has to
get rid of Nicholas—and us—before the
storm ends. What are we going to do, Steve?"

"You may be right," Steve said grimly.
"He knows we saw him through that window right after he stabbed Jennifer. He must
have gone completely crazy to have done
what he has."

"Do you think Eileen knows?" Dee asked,
still whispering.

"I don't know," Steve said softly. "We must
come up with some sort of plan—and we
can't let her know what it is. We'll talk to
Jason and see what he can contribute."

Dee moved around Steve to peer around
the edge of the door at Nick's sleeping form.
"Do you think he'll be all right? Shouldn't
one of us stay with him?"

"He should be safe for a few minutes," Steve said. "While you were fixing his bed, I put everything movable that would make a noise on the window seat beneath the window—even his silver bell. Nobody's coming in that window without making a big racket."

"Then let's go." The two of them hurried down the hall to the living room, to find Gilly and Jason sitting alone like two frozen statues. From the kitchen came the sounds of Eileen as she put away the last of the dinner things.

"How's the old man?" Jason asked anxiously, jumping up when he saw them come in. "Should he be alone?"

"He's sleeping very peacefully right now," Steve said as he sat down, his hands hanging between his knees. "But we have to talk." In a low voice, he began to recount the story Nicholas had told, and his audience listened without interruption.

When he had finished, Gilly looked at him, her eyes wide. "No wonder he didn't want to talk about it," she said. "I'm not surprised that he got so angry with Jennifer."

"Speaking of Jennifer, I think we all know there's a murderer here on this island with us."

Gilly nodded. "Yes. Somehow, with Jennifer gone and all, I realize I've got to finish this assignment myself. I'm not as brave as she, and not as strong—but I'm sitting on a good story, and somehow I want to document it."

"Maybe we can help you, if you help us," Jason announced in a low tone.

"Anything," the girl answered, swallowing nervously. "Just tell us what to do!"

Jason leaned toward her, speaking just loudly enough so that they were all aware of his words. "I think we all know it has to be Bert—and he means to kill Nicholas. The old man is a sitting duck asleep and alone in that bedroom down the hall. If Bert tries to get to him, I'd like a reception committee waiting for him—a committee of one. Me." He paused for a moment. "Naturally, before he tries to break into Nick's room, he'll want to know the whereabouts of the two men in the house—Steve and me. Not that anyone can see much through the shutters."

"What's your plan?" Dee asked tensely.

"When Mrs. Powers comes back in, Gilly should announce that she's tired and frightened and wishes to go to bed. After you leave, Gilly, I'll slip some pants, one of my jerseys, and a pea jacket into the bathroom at the end of the hall. I want Gilly to pretend to be me. She can slip into that bathroom and change in the dark."

"Oh, that wouldn't fool anybody," Gilly said nervously. "I don't look a thing like you!"

"You would, sitting on the couch, with your back toward the shuttered window. Only thing, we'll have to hide that red hair. Maybe if I gave you a cap—but, no, you wouldn't be wearing a cap in the house."

"Jennifer brought some wigs," Gilly said, her eyes lighting as she spoke. "There's a short curly black one that would do fine!"

"Do you have the guts to go into her room and get it?" Jason asked bluntly.

"Oh, my! I don't know! I—"

"It will have to be you—and you'll have to be careful how you get it. Remember, from this point forward, anybody could be looking in the windows. Or trying to look around the shutters. Get it when you get your night clothes."

"I could just take the whole bag," Gilly said doubtfully. "I don't suppose anybody would know it didn't have night clothes in it."

"Right! I'll leave my clothes in the half

bath at the end of the hall. Once you're
dressed for bed, blow out your candle and
make your way to the bathroom in the dark.
I'll get up from my seat on the couch here
by Dee and go into the bathroom myself.
Only, you will come back, not me. I'll put a
couple of extra pillows on the couch to make
you look taller when you sit down. Just be
sure not to turn your face toward the window at any time."

Gilly shuddered. "I'll be sure!"

Steve eyed him keenly. "And where do
you plan to be?"

Jason's eyes held a dangerous glint. "In
Grandfather's room, of course. I have a feeling that Bert will go for him first. The three
of you will be out here together, and he will
think Gilly's in bed. It's worth a shot, anyway."

Dee glanced toward the shuttered windows. "I don't see how he could even stand
up out there, much less do any spying."

"I wouldn't bank on it." Jason got up
abruptly and began to lay a fire in the grate.
"This storm has given him a golden opportunity, and I believe he's going to cash in on
it."

Behind them, the dining-room door
creaked open and Eileen stood there. "Will

you be wanting anything else this evening?" she asked just as though it were an ordinary night.

"Has Bert come in out of the storm?" Jason asked her quietly. "You know he's out there, Mrs. Powers."

"You'd all like to blame him for that reporter's death, wouldn't you? Well, he's not guilty. Bert hasn't done anything, and I'm sure he has taken shelter in his own place until this storm is over and he can prove it." Her eyes flicked from one to another of them, resting briefly on each face. "I wouldn't feel too cozy with each other if I were you. One of you is a murderer, and you know it! You're not going to get away with blaming it on my boy!"

Gilly jumped to her feet nervously. "I can't stand this anymore!" she cried. "I want to go to bed and lock my door and wait for morning to get off this horrible island! Where can I sleep, Mrs. Powers? I certainly can't stay in that room with—with her—"

"I've prepared another room for you," the older woman said calmly. "If you'll just follow me."

Gilly almost ran across the floor to her side. "I have to get my case out of her room.

Will you go with me? I'm afraid."

"I'm sure there's nothing to be afraid of,"
Eileen told her patiently. "Just come along
with me." She headed for the door and turned
when she reached it. "I'll be going to bed
myself after I show Miss Jones to her room.
I'd like to mention that my door has a dead
bolt, so I wouldn't advise any of you to come
visiting tonight."

Gilly followed her out, and Jason returned to his fire-building. As soon as he
had a flicker of flame, he put up the screen,
for strong gusts of wind were finding their
way down the chimney and blowing at the
fingers of fire.

The couch sat along the floor, its back to
the window. Jason casually flung a couple
of pillows on the seat, then sat back in the
firelight. "Come sit beside me, Dee," he ordered. "Steve, you take the easy chair facing
the windows. That way you can try to keep
an eye on the outside."

Dee obediently went over to sit beside
Jason. Only once did he leave for a short
while, and she knew he had gone to transfer
the clothing to the hall bath.

"What do you think will happen?" Dee
asked Jason nervously as soon as he was

back, keeping her voice low and trying not to shiver.

"Nothing, if we're lucky," Jason answered. "But if our murderer is Bert, he'll have to move tonight. I won't be far away — just down the hall with Nicholas. His bath has a second door that opens into the hall, so I can get inside it without being seen from the windows — if anyone can see around the shutters. And if anybody tries to harm him, I'll be waiting for them. They won't get away with it."

"I've never felt more helpless in my life," Dee confessed.

"Try not to worry," Steve counseled her from across the room. "But stay alert. Anything can happen."

"And probably will," Dee answered.

The storm seemed to be gaining in ferocity. Dee heard a trickle of wetness and looked behind her to see that water was forcing its way through the sealed windows, dripping down the walls, and puddling on the floor.

A hiss from down the hall drew Jason's attention. "This is it," he said softly. "Remember — keep Gilly's face masked from the windows, shutters or no."

Jason rose slowly, stretching, turning his head toward the shuttered windows. Somehow Dee felt there were malevolent eyes out there, peering in at them from the frightening storm.

She tried to keep up a running conversation with Steve, but she knew she was uttering banalities. Eyes seemed to be boring into her back, and she wanted more than anything else to scream and run. Somehow she forced herself to sit quietly and wait.

The dark shadow who came back into the room could easily have been Jason. The curling mass of dark hair, the broad shoulders under the blue jersey and pea jacket, the dark trousers. It seemed a real anticlimax when Gilly sat down on the cushions beside Dee, the added height making her almost the same size Jason had been.

"Has Eileen gone to bed?" Steve asked.

Gilly nodded. "And as far as she knows, so have I," she said.

They tried to carry on a conversation as the wind leaked in to blow the curtains, and the puddling water on the floor grew deeper. Once Steve got up to feed the fire, for it was the only light they had except for one flickering candle. Dee knew that, from the outside, anyone—if he could see anything— would believe she was sitting here by the fire with two men, waiting out the storm.

CHAPTER TEN

Dee moved slightly to ease a cramp in her leg. The fire was dying again, and there was very little more wood to feed into its hungry maw. Gilly, disguised as Jason, looked tired and strained, with dark-blue smudges under her eyes.

Dee had begun to suspect that Bert wouldn't make his move tonight. It was very late, well past midnight, and they had been perched here like sitting ducks for hours. She knew she would have to get up soon and move around the room to ease her aching muscles, and she wondered how Gilly could sit so long, her back to the window, careful not to turn her face. The entire farce had been a bad idea.

It was hard to believe that, outside those

windows that were carefully shuttered, something evil lurked that could threaten all their lives. Yet Jennifer's body, stretched out so still in her room, was evidence that it was so. Their enemy had to be almost superhuman to exist outside these walls, where the wild wind and the rain tore about so unmercifully.

Gradually, Dee got the feeling that she could hear something on the edge of her consciousness. It was a different sound from the rest of the banging that was going on from flying objects hitting the house. It was a more controlled sound, as though someone were working to loosen a shutter.

What was Jason doing? How was the old man faring? Dee felt her patience growing more thin with every second that passed.

"I can't take this anymore," she said quietly to Steve. "I'm going to check on Jason and Nick."

"I don't know if that's wise," Steve said softly. "We agreed to wait and do nothing unusual."

"I don't think it would be unusual for me to check on my patient. It would be a perfectly natural reaction. Even if anyone is spying on us, he would expect me to do that."

"Jason is with him."

"But an intruder wouldn't know that—hopefully," Dee answered shortly. "This charade has been going on a long time, and we've heard nothing from Jason."

"Maybe you're right," Steve said at last. "But be quick, and be quiet."

Slowly Dee rose from the couch, stretching her arms and her back before she moved across the dark floor. The hall was like a black cavern, with only the faintest flicker of light coming from the direction of Nick's door to guide her. She groped about, her arms extended before her to feel her way through the pitch blackness. Outside, the wind howled like a banshee, screaming like a wounded soul in torment.

Dee sensed, rather than saw, the figure that suddenly loomed over her in the hall. She had just caught her breath to scream when something exploded against her skull, and she saw puffs of blinding light behind her eyelids as she fell, unconscious, to the hall floor.

She couldn't have been out very long before she regained consciousness. Her cheek was lying against the rough carpet, and her hands were tied behind her, making her shoulders ache. When she tried to call out, she found she was gagged as well.

Fear poured over her, joining the adrenaline already in her bloodstream. Whoever it was, he was in the house already. He knew about the game they were playing, and he intended to pick them off, one by one.

She made a choking sound, deep in her throat, and tried to move away from the danger, but she had no idea which direction that was. She could hear Steve's voice faintly, coming from the living room.

"Dee's been gone too long. I think I'd better check on her."

Gilly's reply was unclear, but she had been told to keep her voice low. Dee tried to make another sound, to warn Steve, to keep him out of this dark hall where the enemy awaited.

Helplessly she heard his footsteps coming nearer, approaching from the living room. She made the choking sound again, trying to warn him.

"Dee!" he whispered. "Dee, are you all right?"

At first she thought Steve had stumbled over her legs in the dark, for he fell over, the weight of his body driving the breath out of her. As she gasped helplessly, trying to get air through her gagged mouth, she realized Steve, too, had been struck by her unknown assailant. She could hear the harsh breathing of a third person as he lifted Steve, twisting his body, trussing him up as he had Dee.

Why didn't Jason hear and come to their rescue? Where was he? Or was this maniac who had attacked them Jason himself?

Dee moaned, heaving, twisting, to get away from Steve's prone body with its dead weight resting upon her. Then she saw the light increase as the shadowy figure opened Nick's door wider and went inside, his body blocking the light for one awful moment.

There was nobody to help them now but frail little Gilly, sitting alone in the living room, under orders not to move under any circumstances.

Dee writhed around, rolling nearer to the door. She had to get in there, had to do something to protect her patient. As she freed herself of Steve's body, he was still a dead weight, and she knew he was unconscious— or worse.

Somehow she managed to reach the door and push it aside with her shoulder. Why was everything so quiet? What was happening in that room?

Dee could see the man leaning over Nick's bed. He was wearing dark clothing, and a ski mask completely hid his features. He had lifted one of Nick's pillows and was holding it in his hands, ready to lower it over the old man's face.

On the window seat, all the noisemakers Steve had placed there were still intact, including the silver bell. The man hadn't used the window to come in. He had been inside all the time!

Dee had managed to get her back against the inside wall and was pushing herself to a sitting position when a second figure burst out of the bathroom and leapt on the intruder's back. Dee could see that it was Jason, and she felt a fierce thrill of joy and relief to know he wasn't the one attacking his grandfather.

The two men surged back and forth, their bodies making elongated shadows in strange patterns on the walls. They crashed against furniture, came together, and fell violently to the floor.

With horror, Dee saw the flash of a knife. The intruder was on top of Jason, straining to put the knife in his throat, while Jason was holding him at bay with all his strength.

A little wail brought Dee's attention to

the door where Gilly stood helplessly wringing her hands. Dee managed to make enough of a sound so that the frightened girl's attention was drawn to her plight.

"Oh, Dee," she exclaimed weakly. "Oh, Dee!"

Dee tossed her head about furiously until Gilly knelt beside her at last and loosened the gag.

"Help him, Gilly!" she cried as soon as her mouth was free. "Help Jason! He's going to be killed!"

"I don't know what to do," Gilly sobbed, tugging ineffectually on the rope that bound Dee's hands.

Dee could see that it was a losing battle. The knife was almost at Jason's throat, and he wasn't going to be able to fend off his attacker much longer. A groan from the hall told her Steve was coming to as well, but there was nothing he could do either. Jason's lips were pulled back from his teeth and his face was a mass of strain as he fought to protect himself.

A glance showed Dee that Nicholas was sitting up in bed, thoroughly disoriented. As soon as he realized what was going on, he grabbed for his carafe and flung it at the struggling men. It missed, shattering on the floor beyond.

The shot that rang out in the crowded room came as a total surprise to them all. Dee's eyes raced to the source of the flash, but she couldn't make out who was standing there in the darkness.

The bullet had struck the intruder in the right shoulder, knocking him up and away from Jason. Jason was astride him now, holding him flat.

The room seemed to light up miraculously as Eileen entered, bearing an old-fashioned oil lamp. "Good work, Bert," she said shortly, and Dee recognized the man who had come to Jason's rescue and done the shooting. It was Bert Powers.

Bert crossed the floor and jerked the intruder to his feet, keeping him well covered with the gun. "I'll take care of him," he said. "You take care of the others, Jason."

In just a moment Dee felt Jason's strong hands over hers as he released her from her bonds and helped her to her feet. She went immediately to Nick's side, settling him back and taking his pulse as Jason disappeared into the hall and came back helping Steve, who was staggering and holding his head.

"What's going on here?" Nicholas roared. "What are you all up to now?"

"That's just what we're going to find out," Jason said angrily. He walked across the floor toward the man in the ski mask, who was hunched over in agony, his hand clutching his wounded shoulder. "And the first thing on the agenda is to find out just who this is!"

He ripped the ski mask over the man's head and was rewarded with a gasp from the onlookers as Paul Kennedy's bright golden hair was revealed.

Steve looked stunned. "Paul! What on earth got into you?"

Paul glared at Bert, his lip curled in a snarl. "You dirty sneak!" he spat.

Bert stared at him belligerently. "You told me nobody would get hurt. You're a liar, Kennedy!"

Steve staggered slightly and leaned against the wall. "Why don't we get out of here to settle this affair? Mr. Wakeford needs his rest."

"I've warned you before not to mollycoddle me!" Nick snapped. "This is my house and my life, and I want to know what's happening here." A look of sorrow entered his eyes. "Paul—Paul!" he said sadly. "What happened to you?"

Paul eased himself into a straight-backed chair, eyeing Bert carefully. "I guess it's all going to come out now, anyway, isn't it?"

"Yes, it will. Would you like to tell me about it?" Nick's voice was quieter, more controlled.

"I told you it wasn't Bert," Eileen said with satisfaction. "I knew it wasn't him."

"He was certainly involved," Paul spat, holding his wounded shoulder. "I'm hurt, Steve. You're a doctor, man. Help me."

"You aren't seriously hurt," Steve said heartlessly. "Let's have an explanation, and then I'll look you over."

"Yes, Paul," Dee said softly. "First, why did you want to harm Nicholas?"

"He was changing his will," Paul said bluntly. "I had always been executor, in addition to handling his business. The new will gave everything to Jason, put him in charge. I had made some bad investments, sent some good money after bad." He winced. "I would have recouped everything, given enough time. But Nicholas was getting nosy, looking into things—"

"I suspected you'd been nibbling at the

accounts," Nick said wrathfully. "Fortunately, it would take a lot more than you've done to ruin me!"

"And you considered your financial misdealings a good enough reason to kill a man?" Dee cried.

"It was my whole future!" Paul protested. "Once it became common knowledge, I would have been ousted from the bar! As long as the old will was in effect, I held the upper hand. I could have covered my tracks, replaced the money, and no one would have ever known. But Nick wouldn't leave it be. He just wouldn't leave it be!"

"And Jennifer Lane? Why did you kill her?"

"She knew. I don't know how, but she put it all together. Nick should never have let her into his files. She told me what she knew, threatened me. If she had ever written that story, it would have been the end of me. She had to die!" Paul stuck out his bottom lip like a belligerent child.

Sighing, Nick turned his eyes to Bert. "Now let's hear what you have to do with this," he said quietly.

Bert looked ashamed. He was having trouble meeting Nick's eyes. "I thought I was protecting you. I knew you were changing your will, and Kennedy made me believe you were cutting me and Ma out of it. That wasn't the real reason I helped him, though. He also made me think Jason was in cahoots with Dr. Winthrop and his nurse to pressure you into changing the will. And that they planned to do away with you. That's why I kept coming to your room, checking on you. We owe you a lot, my ma and me. Nobody's going to hurt you if I can help it."

Eileen shook her head slowly. "Oh, Bert! You were so mistaken! You helped the wrong man."

"I know that now, Ma," he said wretchedly. "I didn't tell you. I didn't want you upset. Kennedy talked me into hitting him over the head that night at the wharf to take suspicion away from him." Bert's finger tightened on the trigger of the revolver he held, until Jason reached out and took it away from him.

"How did Kennedy get back to the island?" Jason asked gruffly.

"I brought him back with me on Sunday night," Bert confessed. "We anchored the launch on the other side of the island, and

we've been here ever since. I just wanted to
keep an eye on things, but Kennedy seemed
to go a little crazy. I couldn't keep up with
him, specially after the hurricane hit."

"So it was Paul who left the pills on
Nicholas's table," Dee said softly.

"What pills?" Bert asked, perplexed. "All
I know is that after the storm got bad, we
holed up in my place. I was watching while
you weatherproofed the house. If you hadn't
done it, I was going to. I was pretty mad,
anyway, because I saw Kennedy cut Jason's
boat loose. That was a dumb idea, I thought.
After that I couldn't do much with him. He
took off, and I went after him. I got to the
broken shutter outside the Lane woman's
room just about the time you found the body.
I had followed Kennedy there and just
missed him. I think you saw me."

"We did," Steve said roughly. "We thought
you had done it."

"It was rough out there," Bert said. "I finally made my way to Ma's window, calling
out so she could let me in. I was wet and
battered, and she made me get into dry
clothes and wait in her place until she fed
you supper. Kennedy must have gotten into
the house by the back door. We didn't put

everything back on it the way we should because we were in a hurry. I fixed it as soon as I was dry, but I guess meanwhile Kennedy managed to get in."

"You made some mistakes, Bert," Eileen said at last. "I told you so once we had a chance to talk."

"At least I got here in time to stop any more killing," Bert said miserably.

"You saved my life, at least," Jason admitted.

"A fool, Kennedy, you've been a fool," Nicholas said bitterly. "Take him out of here and see to him, Winthrop. Then, as soon as this storm breaks, get him off my island. I never want to lay eyes on him again."

Jason prodded Paul mercilessly with the gun. "On your feet, Kennedy. And don't try to pull anything. You can walk. And everybody else but Dee clear out of here. Now."

Slowly, they all filed out of the open door. It seemed very dark again when Eileen took the bright lamp away.

"Do you think you'll need another sedative?" Dee asked her patient.

Slowly he shook his head. "I'll be all right now. I owe you a lot, Dee. You and Jason, too."

"The important thing is for you to get well." She gave him a warm, gentle smile, and then, on impulse, leaned over and kissed his wrinkled cheek. "That's because I love you," she said sincerely.

He colored with pleasure. "Away with you," he said gruffly. "Can't a body get any sleep around here?"

She pulled the covers up but left the candle burning by his bed.

Down the hall, the light from Eileen's lamp shone brightly through an open door, so Dee had no problem knowing where Paul had been taken. When she went into the room, she saw Jason still had the gun trained on the lawyer, and she could see Steve had been at work.

"The bullet went through the shoulder," Steve informed her. "A clean shot. I sterilized the wound and applied a pressure bandage. I've also given him something to make him sleep. Not only will Paul be more comfortable, but it will be easier to guard him if he's sedated."

Dee nodded silently, noticing how handsome and clean-cut Paul still looked, lying on the bed with the white bandage startling against his brown skin. His blue eyes were becoming glazed, his lashes falling over them in sleep.

"What a waste," Dee murmured. "What a waste of a human being."

"I'll take the first shift guarding him," Steve offered. "I have a feeling you two have a lot to talk about."

Jason nodded. "Thanks, Steve."

Dee let Jason take her back to the living room, where the fire was nothing but embers. They could hear Eileen in the kitchen with Bert, and apparently Gilly was there, too. The smell of hot coffee from a thermos wafted through the atmosphere.

"It's over, Dee." Jason slipped his arms about her as they sat on the couch, cradling her head against his chest. She felt the nervous tension beginning to drain away, along with many of the fears and doubts that had tormented her.

"I'm telling you again that I love you," Jason whispered against her hair. "And I'm asking you to be my wife. We both need you—the old man and me."

Dee closed her eyes in utter contentment. "Do you think Steve knows about us?" she asked, loving the feel of his thudding heart beneath her ear.

"Yes. He knows." Gently, Jason lifted her face until her lips were just below his.

The kiss that followed was long and satisfying, healing a lot of old wounds.

The island was still battered and dreary when the police launch left, taking along a handcuffed Paul Kennedy, the plastic-wrapped body of Jennifer Lane, and a revitalized Gilly.

"I feel awful about everything that happened, but I have the story of a lifetime and the pictures to go with it," Gilly told them just before she left. "It could mean a new career for me!"

Steve, Bert, and Jason had rescued the launch from the other side of the island. It was battered but still seaworthy. Bert took Steve back to the mainland in it, to have it repaired and to answer some necessary questions at police headquarters. Nicholas had asked them to go easy on Bert as an accessory because of the way he had come to the rescue and saved several lives.

Steve clasped Dee's hand in parting and looked deeply into her eyes. "I know it's useless to ask you if you really want to stay," he said.

"Yes, it is. But thanks, Steve. Thanks for

everything." She smiled, her eyes twinkling. "You might stop by the little bait shop on the wharf and tell the young lady there that she's lost her bet or whatever. I've decided to stay permanently on Wakeford Island."

Steve asked, "Do you honestly think you can get along with Eileen Powers?"

"Now that I know the truth about her— yes. That lady's been through a lot. Maybe I can even make things a little easier for her."

Steve grinned with a flash of white teeth. "There's no sense in going overboard and trying to make a saint out of yourself."

"No danger," Dee chuckled. "Anyway, I won't always be here. We'll be doing some traveling, I understand."

"Keep in touch." Steve lowered his lips to brush them against her cheek. "And have a good life."

Dee and Jason stood, hand in hand, and watched the launch bearing Bert and Steve pull away from the pier.

Finally, she turned away, surveying the havoc the storm had wrought.

"We have to get busy," she said sensibly. "This mess has to be cleaned up. There's a whole new marriage waiting to start here."

Jason gave her a big hug, laughing exuberantly. "I have a feeling it's going to be the best marriage Wakeford Island ever had!"